Flames of Devotion

Flames of Devotion

OIL LAMPS FROM

SOUTH AND SOUTHEAST ASIA

AND THE HIMALAYAS

Sean Anderson

UCLA FOWLER MUSEUM
OF CULTURAL HISTORY
LOS ANGELES

The Fowler Museum is part of
UCLA's School of the Arts and Architecture

Lynne Kostman, *Managing Editor*
Danny Brauer, *Designer and Production Manager*
Don Cole, *Principal Photographer*

UCLA Fowler Museum of Cultural History
Box 951549
Los Angeles, California 90095-1549

Requests for permission to reproduce material from this volume
should be sent to the UCLA Fowler Museum Publications
Department at the above address.

Printed and bound in Hong Kong by South Sea International
Press, Ltd.

Library of Congress Cataloging-in-Publication Data

Anderson, Sean, 1972–
    Flames of devotion: oil lamps from South and Southeast Asia
and the Himalayas / Sean Anderson.
        p. cm.
    Includes bibliographical references.
    ISBN-13: 978-0-9748729-3-3 (soft cover)
    ISBN-10: 0-9748729-3-8 (soft cover)
    1. Lamps—South Asia—Exhibitions. 2. Art metal-work—South
Asia—Exhibitions. 3. South Asia—Religious life and customs—
Exhibitions. 4. Pal Pratapaditya—Art collections—Exhibitions.
5. Pal, Chitralekha—Art collections—Exhibitions. 6. Lamps—
Private collections—California—Los Angeles—Exhibitions.
7. Lamps—California—Los Angeles—Exhibitions. 8. University
of California, Los Angeles. Fowler Museum of Cultural History—
Exhibitions. I. University of California, Los Angeles. Fowler
Museum of Cultural History. II. Title.
    NK6475.8.A53 2006
    739.5'2—dc22
                                                    2005023508

Funding for this publication and the accompanying exhibition has
been provided by

Mrs. Yvonne Lenart
National Endowment for the Arts
The Pal Family
Manus, the support group of the Fowler Museum

FRONT COVER: Detail of lamp on page 6.
PAGE 1: Detail of fig. 30.
PAGE 2: Detail of cat. no. 15.
PAGE 3: Detail of cat. no. 22.
PAGE 5: Detail of cat. no. 45.
PAGE 6: Lamp. Nepal. 18th century. X2004.6.1; Gift in honor of
Yvonne Lenart's 90th birthday from the Pal Family, Patricia Reiff
Anawalt, Frances L. Brody, Barbara Goldenberg, Eleanor C.
Hartman, Ann Koepfli, Herbert and Margery Morris, Monica
Salinas, Shirley and Ralph Shapiro, Lillian Weiner, and Marion
and Bob Wilson.
    The central figures on this magnificent Newari lamp are Ganesha,
surrounded by an aureole; the rat, Ganesha's *vahana* (symbolic
mount), under the deity's foot; and a spreading multiheaded *naga*.
Bala Krishna (Krishna as a baby) crawls up the lamp's handle.
PAGE 8: Detail of fig. 16.
PAGE 9: Detail of fig. 22.
PAGE 72: Detail of cat. no. 8.
PAGE 112: Detail of fig. 33.
BACK COVER: See fig. A, fig. 21, cat no. 8.

FOWLER IN FOCUS

Flames of Devotion is a Fowler in Focus book.

Ce livre, comme tout ce que j'écris,
est pour Shannon et le numéro vingt-deux.

Lakshmi Maya
Lakshmi maiya utaren teri arati
Barsado ma kripa
Sab ko naiya dukho se tu hi tarati

(O Mother Lakshmi, as we wave this sacred light before
you, we humbly request that you bestow your grace
upon us. Do protect everyone from the sorrow of this
world and bless us.)

. . . .

Prem ka dipa jagake maiya
Arati teri utaren
He jag jyoti kashta nivarini
Har lena andhiyari
Lakshmi maiya utaren teri arati

(As we light the lamp of love in our hearts we perform
your *arati*. O light of the world, remover of all distress,
do destroy the darkness from our lives.)

verses from a *bhajan*, or prayer,
used in performing *arati* in northern India

Contents

Foreword

Early in 2001 Pratapaditya and Chitralekha Pal invited former Fowler Museum director Doran H. Ross and the Museum's curator of Asian and Pacific collections, Roy W. Hamilton, to their home to see a unique and extensive collection of oil lamps and associated objects, mostly made of cast brass, from India and surrounding regions. The Pals had been building this collection of over a hundred lamps for nearly thirty years. With their very generous gift of the collection to the Fowler Museum, we are now able to exhibit the lamps together for the first time and to produce a focused monograph about them.

The enthusiasm of the Pals and their knowledge of the collection, as well as the wonderful diversity and artistry of the lamps themselves, have made this project a special opportunity. As noted, this book accompanies an exhibition of the same name, which is being presented in the fall of 2006 as part of our Fowler in Focus installation series—designed as a changing component of the Museum's new exhibition initiative *Intersections: World Arts, Local Lives*. Each Fowler in Focus installation highlights and celebrates the strengths of Fowler Museum collections. We warmly thank the Pals again for making us the recipients of this distinctive assemblage of oil lamps.

These lamps join the Museum's already large and varied holdings from South Asia. Our collections are not drawn equally, however, from all parts of the subcontinent, nor do they represent all media and time periods. Rather, the Fowler has extensive and valuable research collections of specific types of objects from this part of the world. Foremost among these is a group of stone temple sculptures donated by Harry and Yvonne Lenart; puppets and shadow puppets collected by the late UCLA Theater Department professor Melvyn Helstein; textiles from Gujarat and surrounding areas collected by Vickie Elson; two groups of textile printing blocks donated by David Brown and Sam Hilu; the areca nut cutters that were a bequest from the estate of Samuel Eilenberg; and a group of textiles from Ladakh donated by Daniel Ostroff. Selections from these collections have been featured in exhibitions dating back to *Asian Puppets: Wall of the World* (1976) and *Dowries from Kutch: A Women's Folk Art Tradition in India* (1979). More recently, South Asian material has been featured at the Museum in *Traces of India: Photography, Architecture, and the*

Politics of Representation, 1850–1900; A Mother's Journey: Photographs from Orissa, India, by Tara Colburn; and as part of the pan-Asian exhibition *The Art of Rice: Spirit and Sustenance in Asia.*

It is therefore decidedly fitting that the Pals' outstanding and highly focused collection of lamps comes to reside at the Fowler Museum. We are extremely pleased to present these objects, which are as yet little known in the United States though ubiquitous in India. In addition to the generosity of the Pals, we also would like to thank Mrs. Yvonne Lenart for her gift to underwrite the costs of this publication and for her ever-constant and enthusiastic support of the Fowler Museum and its programs.

Investigating this largely uncharted subject matter has been challenging, and we thank UCLA Art History doctoral candidate Sean Anderson for his efforts first in cataloging the Pal Collection for us and then in researching and writing the fine essay that appears in this book. We are especially appreciative of the time he has devoted to this project given that its deadlines coincided with his doctoral residency at the American Academy in Rome as a recipient of the 2005 Rome Prize as a Fellow in the Humanities. We are also grateful to Dr. Pal himself, a world-renowned scholar and curator of South Asian and Himalayan art, whose insights have enriched this volume.

Our thanks go to the entire Fowler Museum staff for their contributions to this project. As always they have fulfilled their responsibilities to the highest museum standards and are to be commended for their dedication to the work we do. They are all listed at the back of this volume. Special recognition goes to the members of our publications team who have produced this handsome volume: Lynne Kostman, Managing Editor; Don Cole, Photographer; and Danny Brauer, Designer and Director of Publications.

We hope that *Flames of Devotion* is as illuminating for our readers as lamps themselves are when they are lit each autumn for the dramatic rituals of Dipavali, the annual festival of lights.

Marla C. Berns, *Director*
Roy W. Hamilton, *Curator of Asian and Pacific Collections*

Collector's Remarks

PRATAPADITYA PAL

Mine eyes must perform the ceremony of the lamps of love.
Kabir (1440–1518)[1]

The modest collection of lamps that constitutes the subject of this volume was formed over a period of almost three decades beginning in the mid-seventies. The growth of the collection was serendipitous and often limited by financial constraints, as the curatorial salary I earned was not quite princely. While a curator cannot indulge his personal passion for collecting in his own area of expertise, because of the appearance of conflict of interest, the museum for which I worked, though encyclopedic in its collections, did not acquire what is loosely and artificially—if not arbitrarily—considered to be "folk art and craft," as distinct from "fine" or "high" art. This left the area wide open for an aspiring collector to satisfy his personal cravings with limited funds. But why lamps?

As early as I can remember, lamps were a daily part of my life. Even though I grew up in the 1940s and 1950s in Calcutta (now Kolkata), a large city provided with electricity, a votive, oil-burning, open-flame lamp, usually of brass, would be lit every dawn and dusk in my mother's *puja* room in our home. More importantly, I used to watch with fascination as elderly women made the wicks for these lamps from used cotton fabric, tearing it into strips and rolling these on their thighs. This was an old tradition at least in Bengal. The practice also generated the proverb: "There is always the making of the wick in the morning before the lamp is lit in the evening." In other words, there is always a tale behind a story.

Every time we visited a temple, we watched in awe and fascination as the flickering light from a burning lamp danced across the visible face of the deity in the dark shrine chamber. This was a particularly potent sight in temples of Kali, the patron goddess of the Bengalis of Calcutta. No less thrilling for a child was the ceremony known as *arati*, or benediction, that the priest performed every evening in the temple and at important festivals like Durga *puja* at home.[2] This was done by holding a lamp, usually one with five wicks (*panchapradip*; fig. A), by the handle and waving it before the image in swinging, rhythmic—and sometimes frenzied—motion

A.

Orissa, India
20th century
X2001.11.13

The handle at the back would allow this lamp to be held aloft and waved in an *arati* ritual. The inscription on the lamp reads "Upendra," apparently the name of the donor.

B.

Simple clay lamps such as
these, containing only ghee
and a wick, are ubiquitous
in Hindu rituals.

*Photograph by Stephen P. Huyler,
Patna, Bihar, 1989.*

for considerable time to the accompaniment of loud music. A well-performed *arati* is
still a mesmerizing experience.

Most important of all, and the greatest fun for us as children, was the annual
festival—known as Dipavali or Diwali—observed every autumn on the darkest
night of the lunar month of Karttik (October-November). While Kali is worshipped
in Bengal, in the rest of the country the festival of lamps (*diya, dipa, deepa, dipak*)
is dedicated to Lakshmi, the goddess of good fortune and wealth. The most festive
part of the occasion is the lighting of small, earthen lamps in rows around the house,
somewhat similar to the Jewish Hanukkah and modern Christmas with its electric
illuminations (fig. B).[3]

A lamp is an essential part of most religious ceremonies in South and Southeast Asia—for Hindus, Buddhists, Jains, Muslims, and Christians. Burning lamps,
however, is not an inexpensive affair, and provisions must be made for a constant
supply of oil or clarified butter, or ghee (*ghi*), which has always been a precious
commodity. So we read in inscriptions from Kerala in South India to the distant and
now-lost kingdom of Champa in Vietnam of the rulers and the rich making generous
donations for lamps to burn in perpetuity in temples.

An unknown author has spun a charming tale in one of the Hindu sacred
texts to emphasize the merit one accumulates by donating lamps.[4] The story involves
Lalita, born a princess of Videha and the queen of the ruler of Kasi (modern Varanasi).
Lalita was born to royalty because of the act of merit she had performed in her
previous life as a mouse living in a temple. In her mouse incarnation she had once
managed to keep a lamp burning in the shrine even though she was pursued by a cat.
As a result she was reborn in her next life as a princess. As queen she provided for
the lighting of a thousand lamps day and night in a temple of Vishnu. The text does
not tell us how she was rewarded in her next birth for her extravagant generosity, but
such charming Disneyesque tales invite the pious to make lavish gifts to temples.

While I did not read such edifying stories until much later in life, two tales involving lamps captured my youthful imagination. One of these tales was about Tansen, the great musician who graced the court of the Mughal emperor Akbar (r. 1558–1605). He is said to have brought down the rains and started fires by singing particular ragas, or melodies. When he sang the *Mallar*, the rains would come down in buckets. Once when he was forced to sing the raga *Dipak*, or *Lamp* or *Flame* raga, against his wishes, the pavilion caught fire and burned down (apparently this did not constitute arson). This is purportedly why musicians since that time rarely sing this raga, but artists have continued to depict it as may be seen in a sumptuous eighteenth-century picture by an unknown master of Murshidabad in West Bengal (fig. c). The other memorable tale was the exotic account of Aladdin and the magic lamp. I still vividly remember how real the story of that lamp—habitat of the genie—seemed to me when I first read it at the age of ten or so. I used to wonder what my three wishes would be if I were lucky enough to acquire such a marvelous lamp.

This tale is not known in Indian literature, but allusions to lamps are so frequent that one could write an entire book about them. That the lamp symbolizes a lighted tree of life is clearly evident from the use of the expression *dipavriksha*, or lamp-tree (see fig. 16). According to one ancient text, at dusk "one should worship Lakshmi and then place lamp-trees in temples of the gods and at cross-roads, in cremation grounds, on riverbanks and the tops of hills, in houses, courtyards and shops, in cow-pens and hollow trees" (Kumari 1973, 106). The same text provides further details as to how the festival of Lakshmi, or Dipavali, should be celebrated with lamps (Kumari 1973, 107). Not only should a lamp be placed outside the home, at night, for one month, but:

> all the shops should be decorated with festive textiles.
> Then the merchant, adorned and dressed in new
> raiments, should sit in a clean spot illuminated
> with rows of earthen lamps and feast with friends,
> relatives, the brahmans and servants. [Kumari 1973, 108]

Later at night one should sleep in a well-perfumed and beautifully decorated bed surrounded by rows of lamps. This may well be the most elaborate use of lamps to celebrate Dipavali prescribed in a sacred text.

Perhaps the most stimulating aspect of this utilitarian and ritual object for me, however, is its metaphorical use in literature. To begin with, brought up in Bengal and speaking the Bengali language, it was inevitable that I would fall under the spell of the much-adored Bengali poet Rabindranath Tagore (1861–1941)—lyrics such as "My lamp is extinguished in the nightly breeze, / Come, come my friend with gentle steps, do not turn away"; or "My blind lamp stares at the sky/ to communicate its shame to the stars of the disappointed night"; or again, "The clay lamp burns within the humble adobe, / but its light is watched by the distant evening star."[5]

Tagore's frequent use of the lamp both as a poetic conceit and a metaphor has a long history in Indian literary tradition. Perhaps the most well-known is the following verse from the most popular Hindu sacred text, the *Bhagavadgita* (fourth century BCE), where the still flame of the lamp has become a metaphor for the unwavering concentration of an ideal yogi: "As a lamp in a windless place flickereth not, to such is / likened the Yogi of subdued thought, absorbed in the / yoga of the Self" (Besant 1967, 94)

The less widely known but more aesthetic use of the lamp as a metaphor was by the Buddha (sixth to fifth century BCE). In his last sermon to Ananda and his followers, the Buddha made the famous pronouncement:

> Be ye lamps unto yourselves. And whosoever, Ananda,
> either now or after I am dead, shall be a lamp unto
> themselves, and a refuge unto themselves, shall betake
> themselves to an eternal refuge, but holding fast to the
> truth as their lamp, and holding fast as their refuge to the
> truth, shall look not for refuge to one besides themselves
> —it is they, Ananda, among my Bhikkhus [monk followers]
> who shall reach the very topmost Height![6]

Countless such analogical and metaphorical allusions to the lamp can be found in Indian literature. The lamp was a natural choice as it literally dispelled the darkness that enveloped the human being for half his life and metaphorically served as a symbol of enlightenment. Collecting lamps for me was an affordable way to indulge in my addictive proclivity but also an enriching aesthetic and spiritual experience.

Although I did the collecting, the support from my spouse throughout was unstinting. It gives us both great pleasure to share this collection with a wider community of scholars and Museum visitors. We would like to thank especially Mrs. Yvonne Lenart—the Fowler's Lamp—without whose generous support this project would have remained unfulfilled. Thanks are also due to Christopher Donnan, Doran Ross, and Marla Berns—three successive directors of the Fowler Museum—and to Roy Hamilton, the Museum's curator of Asian and Pacific Collections, for their enthusiasm and cooperation.

c.

Dipak ragani

Murshidabad, West Bengal,
  India
18th century
Watercolor and gold on paper
Kapoor Galleries, Inc.,
  New York

---

1. Translated by Rabindranath Tagore and quoted in Alphonso-Karkala (1971), 553.
2. The word *arati*, sometimes spelled *aarati*, is abbreviated from the Sanskrit word *aratrika*, which means, according to Monier-Williams (1979, 150): "The light (or the vessel containing it) which is waved at night [*ratri*] before an idol."
3. Electric lights are also used lavishly in India today in Dipavali, often eclipsing the traditional clay lamps, especially in urban areas.
4. Hazra (1958), 130. The story occurs in the *Vishṇudharmapurāṇa*, chapter 32.
5. Translated from the original Bengali to be found in Tagore (1968), 385, 551, and 586.
6. The passage occurs in the *Mahā Parinibbāna-sutta (The Book of the Great Decease)* as excerpted in Alphonso-Karkala (1971), 238.

Preface

The Fowler Museum of Cultural History is the fortunate recipient of an extraordinary collection of oil lamps and incense burners from South and Southeast Asia. These have been donated by Pratapaditya and Chitralekha Pal, who collected them over several decades. The seventy-six individual metal *puja* (ritual worship) lamps and burners illustrated in this volume form the heart of the one hundred six objects in the Pal Collection. Although a preponderance of the lamps in the collection are from the Indian Subcontinent, a significant number come from Nepal and Tibet and a smaller selection have their origin in Southeast Asia, specifically Cambodia, Java, and Vietnam.

Distinctive for their ingenuity of design and diverse crafting, as well as their iconographic richness, the lamps presented within this book and in the exhibition that accompanies it were made for use predominantly in rituals of benediction and in the making of offerings—both in the home and temple. They have been selected to represent a spectrum in terms of place of origin, manner of use, and historical period. While anthropomorphic Lakshmi *dipa* (lamps) from Tamil Nadu and Rajasthan evoke the utterly feminine attributes of Devi, the generic Hindu term for "Goddess," ornate Tibetan butter lamps and hanging Nepalese architectural lamps accentuate the physicality of places associated with spiritual agency. The materials and workmanship of the lamps further suggest their spiritual and ritual value. From a sensuous use of brass accentuating the subtleties of the human figure to the coarser articulation of animals and the environment, these lamps display the incomparable artistry of urban and tribal craftsmen working largely during the period from the eleventh to the twentieth century. One exception, however, is the rare hanging lamp attributed to the Dongson culture of Vietnam (see fig. 20), which is noteworthy not only for its unusual design but also for its early dating. Another is the intriguing copy of a Roman lamp of indeterminate date that was purportedly found on the Indonesian island of Sumatra (see cat. no. 1).

The lamps illustrated represent fourteen states in India, the majority being from the western states of Rajasthan and Gujarat, the tribal areas in central Madhya Pradesh and Chhattisgarh, and the southern states of Kerala and Tamil Nadu, while a few lamps originate from the Kond tribe in Orissa. In addition, several lamps come from other countries and illustrate the breadth of Hindu and Buddhist artistic transmission throughout southern Asia. It is not always easy to distinguish the religious context of the lamps, however, and one hanging lamp was used in an Islamic setting (see cat. no. 25). Stunning examples from Nepal and Tibet showcase the skill with which precious materials were employed during the eighteenth and nineteenth centuries, while early incense burners and lamps from Cambodia, Indonesia, and Vietnam point to the role these objects played in the ancient imagination. What unifies these lamps from diverse locales and times is a fundamental belief in their promise as agents of devotion.

Although some of their imagery may initially appear commonplace, the lamps can be made to reveal a wealth of secrets. The five types of lamps discussed here offer a glimpse into the complexities of the symbolic and ritual systems that dominate daily life in South Asia. In this book I aim to examine the historical import of the lamp, but I also propose to define the space that lamps occupy between the secular and the sacred. Altar and tool, icon and fine sculpture, the lamp's existence is liminal, and its unique position as an essential component of the quotidian and a vehicle of spiritual practice points to the depths of its significance.

Whether in the smallest village shrine of India or in a temple set amidst the suburban sprawl of North America, the use of lamps remains as much a component of the Hindu and Buddhist ritual code today as it did eight centuries ago. Nowhere is the lamp's symbolic and pragmatic resonance felt more than in the countries of India, Nepal, and Tibet, where it is associated with nearly every event that structures a person's life in the world. The lamp is a primary medium through which a deity is acknowledged, and its design, construction, and use have become synonymous with the faith of the devotee.

This essay attempts to explain how and why lamps have endured throughout the history of South Asia, and why they remain omnipresent in the Hindu and Buddhist consciousness. A discussion of the history and aesthetics of the lamp is of particular importance in the twenty-first century when these items are swiftly succumbing to mass production. Furthermore, despite the lamp's obvious significance and longevity, there is very little published material considering it as an object of fine artistic production. This essay attempts to reveal the underlying significance of the lamp while elucidating its history and aesthetics.

I have approached the lamps in the collection comparatively and have not delineated them according to political and temporal boundaries. This strategy differs from the few published commentaries that exist.[1] In so doing, it is my intention to investigate an array of issues, from the construction and design of the lamps to their representation in ritual contexts. The goal of this study is to allow the lamps to cast their own radiant narratives, thereby illuminating a hitherto unseen dimension of a centuries-old artistic and religious tradition.

Sean Anderson, Rome, 2005

---

1. I rely heavily on the notations of the inveterate collector, scholar, and poet Dinkar Gangadhar Kelkar whose publication of 1961 on the history of lamps in India is the first to examine the lamp as having cut across historical and aesthetic tropes. Kelkar amassed one of the largest collections to date of artifacts and materials from everyday life in India, including lamps. These are on display in his private museum in Pune, Maharashtra, India. There is also brief mention of the lamp in the primary literature of South Asian art history primarily demonstrating the range of metalwork on the subcontinent.

Notes to the Reader

Throughout the text diacritical marks have been omitted from Sanskrit words to facilitate reading. A List of Sanskrit Terms with Diacritical Marks is included at the end of the book. Unless otherwise noted, lamps are cast copper alloy (brass or bronze).

Aknowledgments

The staff and directors of two museums have made this book and exhibition happen. To everyone at the Fowler Museum: *Namaskar!* Foremost, I must thank Fowler director Marla Berns who oversaw all phases of this project. Her commitment to exploring and celebrating the world's arts and cultures has resonated through every conversation I have ever had with her. Roy Hamilton, the Fowler's curator of Asian and Pacific Collections, was a patient guide and editor from beginning to end. I thank him for reading and editing the early drafts of my essay. *Tanti saluti* are due to the Registration Department—including Sarah Kennington, Farida Sunada, Gassia Armenian, and Rachel Raynor—for their boundless patience, infectious enthusiasm, and genuine kindness. My thanks also go to Dr. Stephen Huyler who graciously permitted the use of a number of his beautiful and evocative photographs and to Kapoor Galleries Inc. for permission to reproduce an outstanding *dipak ragani* painting.

In Pune, India, I am especially grateful to the honorary director of the Raja Dinkar Kelkar Museum, Dr. H. G. Ranade, who introduced me to an astounding array of lamps and other materials in the museum's collection. A special mention must also go to Dr. Ranade's son, Sudhanva, who assisted me in obtaining a copy of Kelkar's written works. I also wish to thank the American Academy in Rome, where much of the manuscript was completed. I could not have finished it without the support of my friends in Rome, India, and the United States, in particular Jae Emerling and Amy Pederson.

Finally, I want to express my heartfelt gratitude to Pratapaditya and Chitralekha Pal whose undying pursuit of beauty in all forms continues to be an inspiration: *Bahut dhanyavad* and *Tashi Delek!* Without Pratap's unwavering support and dedication, this book and exhibition would never have come to pass. I am extremely fortunate to have Dr. Pal as my teacher and am indebted to him for the knowledge he has shared with me over the years. As always, my love and affection is given to my family who allowed me go to India for the first time without ever asking why.

Sean Anderson

Flames of Devotion

When night descends on the Indian Subcontinent, ceremonial bells are rung in the temples to mark day's end. Distant voices emanate from minarets, and chants from unseen interiors linger in the air. Familiar places shed their comfortable luster. Footsteps lose distance and vigor. Spaces close in as they are embraced by shadows. As autumn approaches and the days grow shorter, a host of events mark the Hindu calendar with brilliant displays of light to dispel the unknown and to encourage a beneficial new year. The gods have been sleeping the past several months and are now ready to be awakened. Streets and houses are cleaned. Fields are returned to dormancy. Colorful new foil bedecks altars and icons. Equally important are the numerous rituals performed inside the home and temple that employ the flame of a lamp. The significance of such displays lies in the interaction between the individual and light itself.

Sometime between the life of the Buddha (sixth to fifth century BCE) and the birth of Christ, Buddhists, Jains, and Hindus began to dedicate lamps in shrines. The appearance of lamps in ancient literature, however, suggests that they performed their roles as devices of commemoration and utilitarian implements long before this period. Perhaps even more significant is the continued use of lamps in a plethora of distinctive forms throughout South and Southeast Asia as well as among South Asian communities around the world.

By virtue of its light and heat, the lamp—usually fabricated in metal or clay—is conceived as the vehicle through which the divine can be accessed. Lamps are used in rituals within the domestic realm, as well as religious or temple settings, in order to propitiate the gods. There are innumerable ways in which lamps are employed depending on the specific location and society.

During the countless festivals that punctuate the Hindu and Buddhist years, the lamp plays a pivotal role as a mechanism that allows the faithful to focus their concentration on the image or nature of the deity. Within the more private setting of the home, the lamp is used in Hindu practice to activate the presence of the deity with the *arati* ritual—the moving of a lamp, held on a plate, in a circular fashion in front of an image (fig. 1). This allows the devotee to acknowledge and to accept

1.

A Hindu priest performs the *arati* ritual every day at dusk. Standing at the river's edge, he holds a large multitiered cast-iron lamp. Accompanied by chanting and the ringing of ceremonial bells, he moves the lamp in a circular motion as darkness descends.

Photograph by Stephen P. Huyler, Varanasi, 2000.

blessings. While the form of the lamp changes, depending on the religious context in which it is made and used, it is the lamp's "carrying" of light that is significant, whether it takes the form of a goddess, an animal, or a tree. The preservation of light signifies the deity's favor and presence. An intersection of the human and the divine is thus central to the crafting of the lamps and incense burners under consideration. While building upon a number of noteworthy objects from the Pal Collection, *Flaming Devotion* attempts to illustrate that the lamp continues to be an evocative reminder of an undying devotion forged with the most common yet enigmatic of materials—metal and light (figs. 2, 3).

EARLY HISTORY AND LITERARY EVIDENCE OF THE LAMP IN INDIA

Since earliest recorded history, fire and light have provided the basis for tales of devotion and of the spirit of humankind. Representing life and its potential, light was believed to signify man's direct relationship to the universe and its creator. The light of the sun was a force that insured the continuance of life.

For most of South Asia, and especially India, light is symbolized by the interlocking forces of two ancient gods, Surya and Agni. Perhaps the most important deity of ancient Vedic literature (ca. 1500 BCE) is Surya or Aditya, the sun.[1] Surya is considered to be the embodiment of the triumvirate formed of the gods Brahma, Vishnu, and Shiva and to correspond to the three phases of the morning, noon, and evening.[2] According to the Vedic texts, the sun sustained life and was thus considered to be a repository of endless energy and power. Through Surya, the followers of Vedic religion were afforded continued security and material prosperity during the day.[3] When night fell, however, the embodiment of the sun was relinquished to Agni, the fire god.[4] The *Rigveda*, the earliest canonical Brahmanic text, stresses the importance of Agni as a transformative deity, carrying the purified sacrificial offerings to the other gods. Since Agni brought warmth and comfort in the face of the enveloping darkness, he was thought of as an ever-present protector, visible throughout the land as a guide and *sakshin*, or witness. He was, as he is today, invoked as a mediator (*duta*) at life-cycle ceremonies (*samskara*) such as births, marriages, and deaths. Agni continues to be inextricably associated with human life as the only deity called *griha-pati* (lord of the house); he is also commonly referred to as *atithi* (guest in the home). The sun and its earthly surrogate, fire, are regarded as the most powerful of healers, remedying disease and bringing life. In addition to the domestic hearth, which provided heat and light, the humble lamp also supplied illumination. This union of heat and light as a source of life was conceived of as the universal nucleus from which all knowledge sprung.

What emerges from the canonical texts is the notion that an inimitable life force drives the universe—its creation and destruction. This energy is referred to as *jivanjyoti*, "the flame of life." While there is no specific mention of the lamp in Vedic literature, by the time of the sutras and epics (approximately the time of the Buddha, sixth to fifth century BCE), two words had come to signify the lamp: *pradip*

2.

Nepal
17th century
X2001.11.101

This donor lamp is made to resemble a kneeling man. It has four burners and a wooden stand. An inscription in seventeenth-century Newari script is no longer legible, although it presumably names the donor and the temple to which the lamp was donated.

3.

Nepal
19th century
X2001.11.103

This donor lamp takes the form of a standing devotee wearing traditional Nepalese dress. A single burner is located atop the figure's head

4.

Nepal
18th century
X2001.11.99a,b

This lotus lamp has a stand and
a triangular base. A removable
peacock finial surmounts the
lamp, and at its base are three
burners, each positioned in
front of an image of the Hindu
deity Ganesha.

and *dipak* or *dipa*, which come from the root *dip*, meaning "shine" or "luminous." Furthermore, ancient Indian philosophers used various incarnations of the lamp to elaborate upon the congruent nature of self and other. In epic literature such as the *Mahabharata* and the *Ramayana*, the lamp, encrusted with jewels and precious materials, is expounded upon as fulfilling the gift of life. The lamp appears as a metaphor for life or for the self—as well as for wisdom and knowledge—in numerous other ancient literary contexts as well (see Collector's Remarks, pp. 13–17).

Within the sanctum known as the *garbha-griha* (womb chamber), the most sacred, and often the darkest, space within the Hindu temple, the flame of a single lamp is used to illuminate all other lamps within the precinct. In an article on lamps from South India written in 1916, O. C. Gangoly suggested that the presence of lamps within the inner sanctum of the temple "not only produce[s] the 'dim religious light' which stimulates devotion, but is indispensable for guiding the footsteps."[5] Individuals who partake of the all-encompassing energy source or "flame of life" resemble lamps lit from the single source in the interior of the temple. Light, and symbolically its bearer, the lamp, can thus perhaps be regarded as progenitors of the individual soul (*atma*)—unbroken in life and death, emanating from an eternal source. Lamps are lit to celebrate the evolving presence of this life force. Throughout the course of daily existence in South Asia—be it in a darkened temple, in the family home, or on a taxi driver's dashboard—the ubiquitous lamp serves as a bridge between the sacred and the profane.

ARCHAEOLOGICAL EVIDENCE

While archaeological excavations at sites of early civilizations in India and Pakistan have not to date produced incontrovertible evidence of actual lamp use, by the second century BCE we start to see lamps depicted in reliefs in Buddhist contexts. The earliest example is perhaps a railing-panel relief medallion from a Buddhist stupa in Bharhut (located between Jabalpur and Allahabad in Madhya Pradesh), which is sometimes identified as "The Dream of Maya" (fig. 5).[6] It depicts the Buddha's mother lying on her side on a bed or platform. A metal or clay floor lamp with a stand appears near her, its primary purpose being to indicate that the scene takes place at night. It is likely that similar lamps were used in shrines. Lamps also appear in early Gandharan Buddhist reliefs (from present-day Afghanistan, Pakistan, and northern India), and it is theorized that the freestanding columns often seen in early Sri Lankan stupas may have carried lamps. Evidence for the use of lamps is also found on terra-cotta plaques at the legendary site of Chandraketugarh north of Kolkata in West Bengal.[7]

Between the ninth and twelfth centuries CE, major sites such as Borobudur in Java and Angkor Wat in Cambodia, as well as across India, for example at Madurai in Tamil Nadu, all had systems for lighting the exteriors and interiors of structures with lamps. At the sacred pilgrimage site of the Padmanabhaswami Temple in the town of Thiruvananthapuram, Kerala, a long corridor (*sribalipura*) is flanked by stone

pillars into which female figures have been carved, each bearing a lamp in her upraised palms.[8] One might in fact argue that these massive complexes were conceived as immense lamps, drawing the faithful to their interiors where knowledge was conveyed in the presence of light.[9]

MAKING THE LAMP

An oil lamp has a fundamental architecture: it requires a cup to contain oil and a narrow passage or channel to hold a wick. The devotional and symbolic significance of this simple, utilitarian object have, however, led to a tremendous diversity of styles and the development of an elaborate iconography so that the lamp, in addition to its necessary components, has frequently come to have a sculptural quality as well. The first and most common material for making lamps for the masses was almost certainly clay, fired or unfired. Naturally, such lamps would deteriorate over time, but it is still customary in India for village potters to make clay lamps, which are used in abundance at festivals (as will be discussed below).

The majority of the lamps in the Pal Collection were crafted in brass, a metal alloy used on the subcontinent for over two thousand years. From region to region, however, the metal ore available, its quality, working techniques, and local aesthetic preferences differed. While there may be little iconic difference between a Lakshmi *dipa* made in Rajasthan and another in Tamil Nadu, their materials and methods of production affect their ultimate character. Splendid temple lamps from the Kathmandu Valley in Nepal are unusual in that they physically reference the deities, including Ganesha (fig. 6), while lamps used in western Nepal are considerably simpler. Sophisticated Tibetan Buddhist lamps are remarkable for their use of precious

6.

Nepal
18th century
X2001.11.102

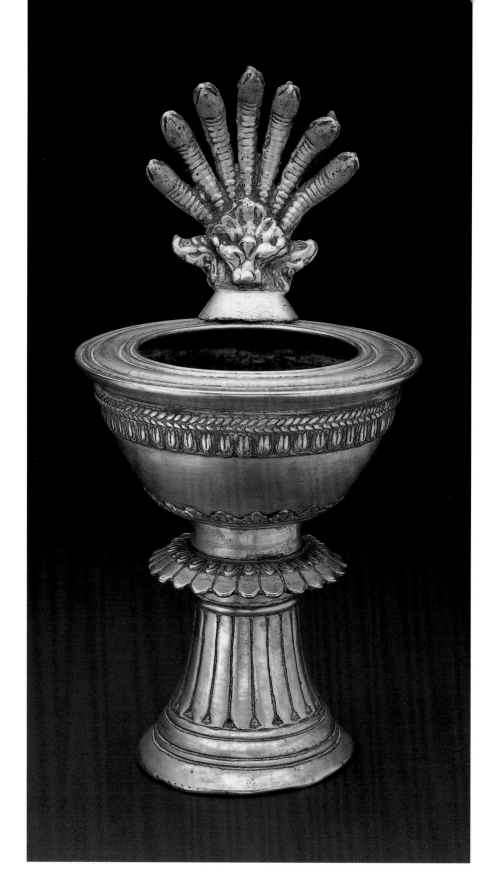

7.

Nepal
18th century
X2001.11.100

This lamp takes the form
of a cup with a stem. It is
surmounted by a finial composed of seven hooded snakes.

metals such as gold, copper, and silver, most commonly the latter (see fig. 11), as well as for their chalice-like form, suggestive of Western influences (see below). Further, while lamps used in India and Nepal burn oil or ghee, Tibetans employ yak butter.

Inventive gestures are apparent throughout the range of objects in the collection, from lamps crafted in the tribal areas of central India to those made by artists in urban settings. The lamp transcends these divisions. With few exceptions, the lamps considered here were created using the labor-intensive method of brass and bronze casting known as "lost-wax," or *cire perdue*. Fundamental to the hollow-cast variant of this technique is the use of an original model in clay that approximates the final image. After this clay model dries, a smooth layer of wax is applied to it. This pliable wax coating permits the artist to create intricate designs (see cat. nos. 2, 17, 18, and 45). A second clay mold is then made over the wax-covered clay core, and a hole is left into which the molten metal can ultimately be poured. Once the metal is poured into the mold, the layer of wax immediately dissipates, and the molten metal replaces it. The external mold is then removed to reveal the object initially crafted in clay and wax. This complex process is still used today.

Among the lamps in this volume, the distinction between tribal or folk crafts and fine sculpture is often blurred, except when we examine their differing methods of production, which include the articulation of decorative patterns and designs. Lamps from the Bastar region in Chhattisgarh and neighboring Madhya Pradesh are a case in point. Renowned art and architectural historian Stella Kramrisch has described the assembly of lamps and other objects by the Bhil and various tribes of northern and central India, who are now referred to as *adivasi* (meaning "original inhabitant").[10] According to Kramrisch, various forms of the lost-wax casting process, have been continually practiced by a nomadic caste of metalworkers, originally from Bengal and Bihar, who are known as the Kainkuya Mal or Dhokra.[11] For instance, metalworkers within groups such as the Malar, having now settled in the state of Bihar, and the Hindu metalworkers (Gharuas or Ghasaias) of the Bastar regions of Madhya Pradesh (a portion of which is now the state of Chhattisgarh)[12] are known to have perfected a technique that allows for the creation of a uniformly ribbed surface. There are a number of instances whereby the lost-wax technique was modified to create idiomatic surfaces, patterns, and imagery. Among lamps from the Bastar tribal regions in particular, the use of specialized casting techniques allowed for complex surfaces. Perhaps not as sophisticated in outward appearance as lamps from more urban areas, the Bastar works are prized not only for their use of highly localized metallurgical processes but also for their whimsical and spontaneous forms. According to Carol Radcliffe Bolon and Amita Vohra Sarin, "Bastar craftsmen use beeswax, which is more pliant and easier to flatten than the resinous substance (*dhuna*) used by the craftsmen of other areas."[13] Such innovations supplement the dimensional quality of the Bastar lamps (see cat. nos. 4, 9, and 10).

The Bastar wax-thread technique, like the more common lost-wax process described above, begins with the making of a clay mold that is covered with wax.

The method of fabrication then differs, however, in that it involves a large number of narrow "threads" that are formed by pressing wax through a wooden tube known as a *pichki farni*. The craftsman covers the surface of the clay and wax mold with these threads, which are pressed against one another, creating "involved and inventive"[14] designs. The threads can also be arranged on the surface to create decorative patterns such as whorls and zigzags.[15] One common decorative trope is the repetition of spirals that are suggestive of eyes or of motifs employed in jewelry and fabric design. The geometric patterning on one Bastar container and incense burner (fig. 8) follows the form of a peacock with an outstretched tail. This augments an already dynamic, as well as functional design that employs a smaller peacock for a lid. Such intricate striated areas often contrast with wide swaths of unarticulated surface and suggest ties to more ancient methods of weaving and basket making in India.[16] Interestingly, an increased demand for these unusual wares has resulted in instances of their mass production. It is now possible to find multiple copies of these once-rare lamps in tourist markets across the subcontinent.

The role of the craftsperson's vision in creating the lamps should not be forgotten. A redefinition of celestial or deified beings in liquefied brass or bronze remains dependent upon a human agent, and the materials and the forms created are seriously regarded. Writing of the reverence that metalworkers displayed for the prescriptions in classical canons regarding their work, Jaya Jaitly notes the belief "that while [the metalworker] is a creator, the energy, strength and inspiration come from divine sources which are translated by the scriptures into precise measurements, proportions, details and even auspicious timings to begin work."[17] Based upon the reading of an early Buddhist source, Ananda Coomaraswamy indicates that the deities depicted on lamps may have been in turn constructed in accordance with a measuring system based upon segments of the human body.[18] Thus the lamp in yet another way becomes a locus for the intersection of the human and the divine.

TYPES AND MOTIFS OF THE LAMP

The lamp serves multiple functions within the temple as well as the home, and its design must befit its placement and use. Among the lamps in the Pal Collection, five primary types emerge. The first of these, the lamp as container incorporates a reservoir for oil and can also bear incense and other perishable materials. As a portable icon, it can also serve as an integral facet of prayer and devotionals. A second group, the *dipa stambha*, facilitates the lighting of larger spaces and events, such as temple assemblies or lectures and school activities. A third type of lamp, the Lakshmi *dipa*, was used primarily within the domestic realm. Such lamps are generally known as *samai*, a name deriving from the Persian word for lamp, *sama*. They tend to display a higher degree of craftsmanship when they incorporate incarnations of Devi, generally in the form of Lakshmi. The fourth, and smallest, group of lamps within the collection is composed of those that hang from chains. The chain lamp was also used to illuminate vast spaces and was commonly suspended from arched windows and doors, as well

8.

Bastar, Chhattisgarh, India
20th century
X2001.11.46a,b

33

as roofs. *Arati* lamps, the fifth type, account for the largest segment of the collection. They are also the most varied in terms of stature and imagery. These, of course, are the lamps used for the *arati* ritual previously described.

Container Lamps: Repositories of Wonder

In fable and myth, the lamp has long been conceived of as a repository of the marvelous, the most famous example being Aladdin's lamp, hiding within it the mercurial genie. Given this "interior life," we might consider how the form of these container lamps serves as an indicator of their dual role as devotional markers and articles of everyday use. A floor lamp from Kerala (fig. 9) is emblematic of this type. With its attached ladle, the low-slung lamp includes a deep reservoir and a cantilevered top plate with shallow burner and a shaped handle or offering area that is subtly engraved with iconic imagery. The lines one sees on the edge of the plate suggest a link to the deity Shiva as they resemble the deity's implement of choice, the *trishul* or three-pronged staff.

A more complex container lamp from Nepal (fig. 10) is also easily recognized as a pitcher for oil with an equally sophisticated ladle. Composed of cast and hammered metal, the highly articulated design of this lamp and oil pitcher imparts a sense of grandiosity and ritual importance. Situated on a simple round base, the lower register of the bulbous basin features an up-turned lotus petal motif—seen on many items in the collection—which mirrors the sixteen down-turned lotus petals in the register above it. While the bottom petals are wide, the upper petals, shown with organic pendants at their intersections, are much narrower. The pitcher gradually tapers to a narrow neck and decorated lip. The lip is thinly inscribed with a snake-scale pattern that is an elaboration of the one seen on the serpent who forms the pitcher's handle.

The expressive serpent, or *naga*, handle is remarkable for its size and apparent realism. The body of the *naga* is incised with generous scales except along its belly, which forms the interior surface of the handle. The serpent's placid face contrasts with its fearsome outstretched hood, which looms above the open container. The inner side of the hood has been realized with linear patterns and stippling while the facial features are lightly delineated.

On the side of the lamp opposite the serpent handle is a large teardrop-shaped burner/reservoir. This is surmounted by a finely articulated figure of the elephant-headed deity Ganesha framed with an aureole. His *vahana*, or symbolic mount, a rat, appears at his feet.[19] Destroyer of obstacles and source of good luck, Ganesha is one of the most popularly worshiped deities in the Hindu pantheon. As he is almost always honored first in rituals, it is not unusual to see images of Ganesha on lamps. This assemblage, which figures prominently on lamps in the collection (see cover), can be seen as an altar unto itself. A *yaksha*, a type of autochthonous nature god, appears below the burner/reservoir, as if supporting it, and contrasts with the fragile yet dimensional aureole poised delicately behind Ganesha. Marked by the presence of deities, the lamp container is recognized as a vessel for divine transactions

that encourages the vigorous recall of a mythic past. With each use, the lamp confirms itself as a site for the instantiation of widely held belief systems.

While functioning primarily as lamps, a number of other objects in the Pal Collection serve multiple purposes. A seventeenth- or eighteenth-century butter lamp from Tibet (*cho-kung*) would have had several functions amidst a temple or monastic setting (fig. 11). Within the sanctums of Tibetan Buddhist religious structures, hundreds of small lamps are filled with clarified yak's butter into which wicks are placed, much as is done on the Indian Subcontinent. This lamp's extensive detailing and precious materials are indicative of a wealthy donor. The reflectivity of the silver would have provided additional color and light in an otherwise darkened interior. It is also important to note that this lamp's shape, like that of many of the Tibetan lamps in the collection, is a distinctive chalice, resembling those used in Western religious settings. Pratapaditya Pal has indicated that such formal appropriations most probably originated from the presence of Nestorian Christians in Central Asia during the eighteenth and nineteenth centuries. Pal also concludes that no lamps of this form are used in Indian Buddhist temples; they are seen only in a Tibetan context.[20] The refinement with which this lamp has been fabricated indicates that the craftsmen responsible for such objects diligently strove to attain greater merit, demonstrating their sincere devotion with their exquisite workmanship.

9.

Lamp with oil container and spoon

Kerala, India
18th–19th century
X2001.11.84

10.

Lamp with oil container,
ladle, image of Ganesha,
and a handle in the form of
a cobra

Nepal
18th–19th century
X2001.11.25a,b

In Nepal lamps of this type
with an attached oil container
are known as Sukundi.

A significant amount of silver was used to create the lamp's florid multilayered
base, which supports a deep, wide reservoir. The craftsman was familiar with the
casting and hammering processes that would be used in figural sculpture of the
region during the eighteenth and nineteenth centuries.[21] A repetitive wave pattern
with cloud-like overlapping curls, a common motif in the Tibetan artistic repertoire,
appears around the circumference of the very bottom of the base. Two rows of
ascending "petals" can be seen as one large lotus blossom; when inverted to function
as a wick snuffer, the lotus blossom can be seen as an upright bloom. The finest
details, however, are seen in the uppermost register of the base where a collection of
leaves and blossoms congregate. Such a focus on the organic seen within an otherwise
stoic container is emblematic of the evolution of nonfigural Tibetan arts.

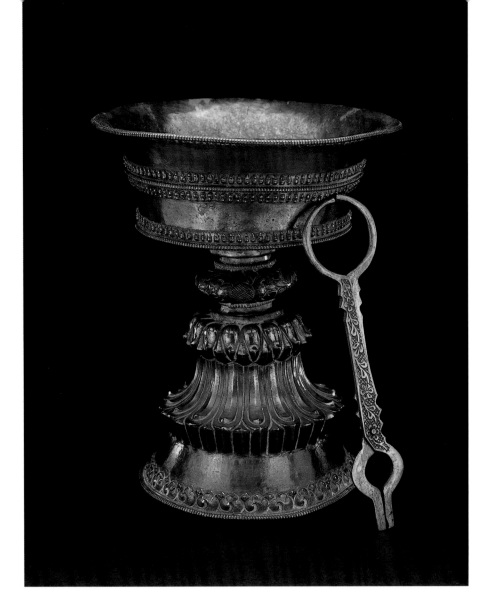

11.

Butter lamp with wick snuffer

Tibet
17th–18th century
Silver
X2001.11.96a,b

The Dipa Stambha: *Trees of Light*

The natural world and the divine meet in the sculpture of South and Southeast Asia, as epitomized in the lamp type known as the *dipa stambha* (*stambha* meaning "pillar"), which is used to illuminate large spaces. The *dipa stambha* has been interpreted in a variety of ways. In an essay on Indian metalwork, Coomaraswamy observed that the most common type of temple lamps are those "standing lamps in the form of a branching tree, each branch ending in a little bowl for oil and wick."[22] Within Hindu spiritual life—as cultural anthropologist Stephen Huyler has noted—the tree is typically synonymous with a specific locale that is viewed as the bastion of the *grama-devata*, the female deity who encompasses the entire community and is associated with nature and guardianship (fig. 12).[23]

12.

A priest lights numerous ghee-filled lamps at the base of a sacred tree every evening.

Photograph by Stephen P. Huyler, Ochira, Alappuzha District, Kerala, 1996.

13.

Lamp stand

Nepal
19th century
X2001.11.80

14.

Lamp in the form of staggered pots with a cobra finial

Kerala, India
18th–19th century
X2001.11.86a-c

The cobra-headed finial of this lamp screws onto the upper pot, which in turn screws onto the next pot. Small oil burners, which were once attached in rows around the lower pots, have been removed.

    While, as will be shown below, some *dipa stambha* take the form of trees, literally or symbolically, "others are simply upright stands," according to Coomaraswamy, and support "a shallow bowl arranged for several wicks; and very frequently the central rod ends in a bird finial, typically a hamsa bird (swan) or a peacock."[24] Emblematic of South Indian style lamps, a tall stand surmounted by a lamp with a bird perched at its summit is more commonly known as a *hamsa* lamp. O. C. Gangoly has described the sacred associations of this particular bird (actually a gander and not a swan), which is the sacred vehicle, or *vahana*, of Brahma and a symbol of wisdom. The author suggests that the bird itself connotes "fire" and "light," which are in turn associated with Brahma. He continues, "It also sometimes signifies beautiful movement.... [standing] for the beautiful and the auspicious, and thus enjoys precedence before all other animals."[25]

    The Nepalese lamp/candle-holder (fig. 13) in the Pal Collection is an example of a *dipa stambha* made in the form of a stand. One intriguing variant from Kerala is a vessel formed of three interlocking, lamp-encrusted bowls or pots (fig. 14). Devotees carry these lamps in fulfillment of personal vows. The light from the individual reservoirs on the bowls would be symbolically protected by the hooded cobra that surmounts them.

    Two lamps from South India offer differing interpretations of flora and fauna. The first is a large, finely wrought brass stand surmounted by an upright gander on a pedestal. A shallow circular reservoir with petal-shaped spouts allows for ease of

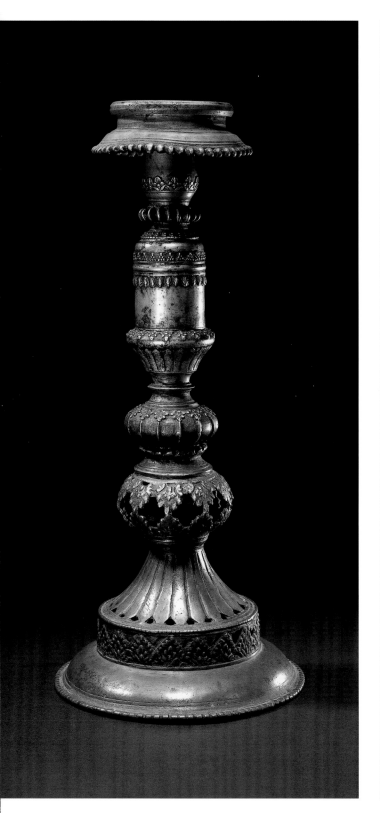

pouring and collecting oil for the lamp (fig. 15). Wicks for the lamp would have been placed along this channel. Along the edges of the pan, between the individual petals, are ten decorative droplets also intended as lotus petals. The physicality of these shapes would seem to heighten the fleeting nature of the numerous flames that would have been lit in the reservoir. It is the auspicious gander that is the most referential aspect of the lamp, and each section of its body is elaborately inscribed with designs.

The second lamp (fig. 16) is a more literal representation of a sacred tree.[26] This extraordinary lamp, a type known as a *vriksha stambha* (*vriksha* meaning "tree"), is complex in its design and construction, based upon a series of numbered pieces. A star-shaped base is embedded with five shallow teardrop-shaped burners and five additional burners held aloft in the outstretched arms of five female figures distinguished by their calm facial expressions. A large elephant with prominent tusks stands at the center of the base, its trunk lowered and mouth open. A small three-ringed design appears at the center of the pachyderm's forehead. On the top of its head are two raised lotus patterns, each composed of six petals. A series of patterns have been inscribed along its back to indicate a ceremonial saddle or patterned textile.

From the center of the elephant's back a cylindrical stand rises, which is sectioned into three zones with eighteen detachable components. The base of this "tree" includes four unidentifiable visages while its crown is adorned with the bust of a female whose sharply defined topknot forms the pinnacle of the whole construction. Below her diminutive face are five shallow burners that include a pointed trifoliate design in the ladling areas. The six burners that appear on each of the three tiers below this are configured identically. Each burner is constructed in the form of a shallow teardrop with six indentations and attached to an armature of paisley design. Within the smaller paisley structure is yet another florid creation of intertwining branches and figures. A small peacock with a raised tail stands above each burner. Behind the tail feathers of each, forming the widest part of the armature, is foliated openwork with multiple spirals and ridges that act as a lyrical continuation of the peacock's plumage. With its intricate numerical foundation and plentiful natural references, the *vriksha stambha* appears to be an instance of the tree cast as Devi, the "Goddess," herself, bearing in her hands the light that portends prosperity for the individuals in a community.

There are also a number of smaller but equally complex *stambha* lamps from the Bastar region in the collection (see cat. nos. 9, 10). Used in smaller quarters, or otherwise venerated within a sacred precinct, these lamps are often enlivened by birds that perch upon the upper oil reservoirs and stands. This lively imagery is not, however, worshipped directly by the Hindu Gharuas, or metalworkers, who create it because it does "not represent their own gods."[27] What we see in this instance is the merging of tribal religion and mainstream Hindu practice. The Hindu craftsmen create works that will potentially resonate with what is most important to the Bastar, the Earth and the feminine presences of the Village Mother and Danteshwari, a hybrid form of the goddess Durga and a "further example of the reciprocity between Hindu

15.

Columnar lamp with auspicious gander (*hamsa*) finial

South India
18th century
X2001.11.24a,b

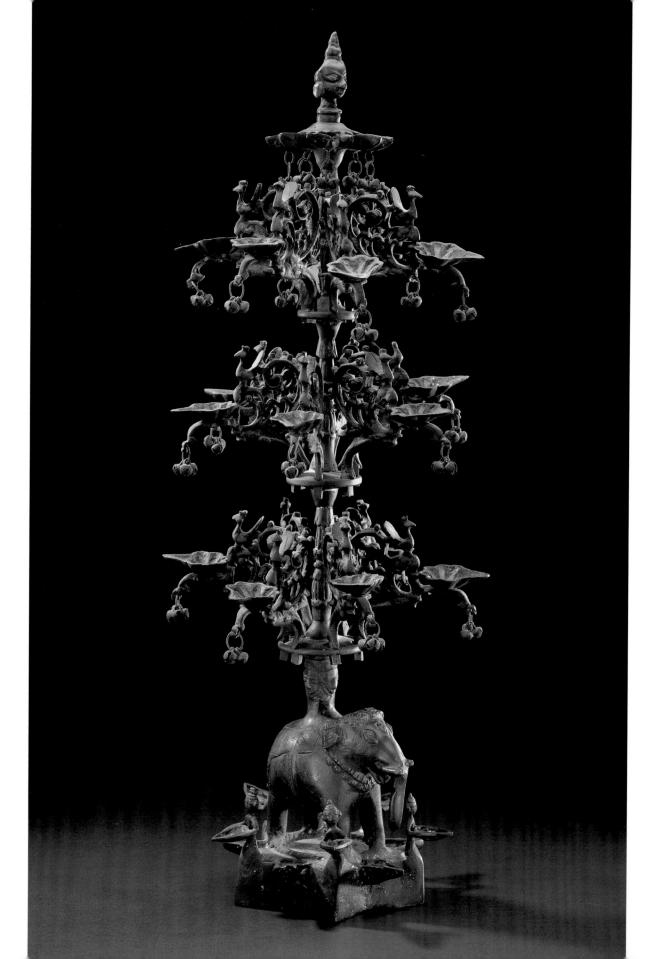

and tribal religious systems."[28] These *stambha* are distinguished not so much for their overall form, which may be seen repeatedly among other lamps from the region, but for their geometric patterning covering nearly every surface and attesting to their tribal origins.

The Lakshmi Dipa: A Feminine Divine

Throughout South Asia countless devotees focus—lamp in hand—upon a female deity generically known as Devi. While Lakshmi and other goddesses have an individual status, they are all manifestations of Devi, who is a sort of *magna mater*, or great mother, figure. The incorporation, manipulation, and evolution of the human figure in the ornamentation of the lamp are fascinating topics of study. One might argue that outside artistic influences, such as those brought to India by the ancient Yavanas, or foreigners, operating in and around the subcontinent, spurred the use of the human figure within circles of indigenous artisans. Local craftsmen adapted this format utilizing postures, facial features, clothing, and jewelry with which they were familiar. Although sensuality is not necessarily characteristic of the design of common lamps, it is often conveyed when Devi is represented.

Variations in use of the human figure among the lamps in the collection allow for a comparative study of regional expression. One dramatic lamp from southern India (fig. 17) features an elegantly attired woman who connotes the goddess Lakshmi. The divine elephant on which she stands is referred to as Sri-Gaja in prayer but is also known as Megha, which means "cloud." Although commonly associated with Indra, the king of the gods, in early Hinduism, it is believed that when this divine animal is invoked, it can summon the winged elephants (clouds) from the atmosphere to visit the earth with their beneficial rainfall. In addition Lakshmi is often portrayed in figural sculpture and two-dimensional works as standing on a lotus flower being lustrated by elephants. This again suggests the arrival of rain and the bringing of life-giving water to the fields. Lamps of this type depicting Lakshmi on the back of an elephant are often given to newlywed daughters-in-law at festival time to ensure their fertility.

Two other striking variations of the female figure come from southern and northern India respectively. The first demonstrates a more sumptuous articulation of bodily attributes and patterning. It is known as the *pavai vilakku* (lit., "lady with a lamp") style and originates from Tamil Nadu (fig. 18). Atop a circular pedestal, the voluptuous figure of a classically proportioned female, Lakshmi, stands proudly holding a deep reservoir/burner in her outstretched hands. Her body arises fluidly and elegantly from the base. Her feet are hidden, covered by her sari, the lower portion of which is embellished with multiple seams and folds accentuated by deep incising. Along the back of the figure, the tight garment accentuates the female form by gathering at a wide central seam that descends from waist to feet. This seam appears as the continuation of a long braid of hair that meets it. Horizontal patterning seen along the folds of the sari indicates the southern origin of the lamp. A short-sleeved blouse,

16.

Tree of life supported on an elephant and featuring animal and human devotees

Andhra Pradesh, India
18th century
X2001.11.23a-t

43

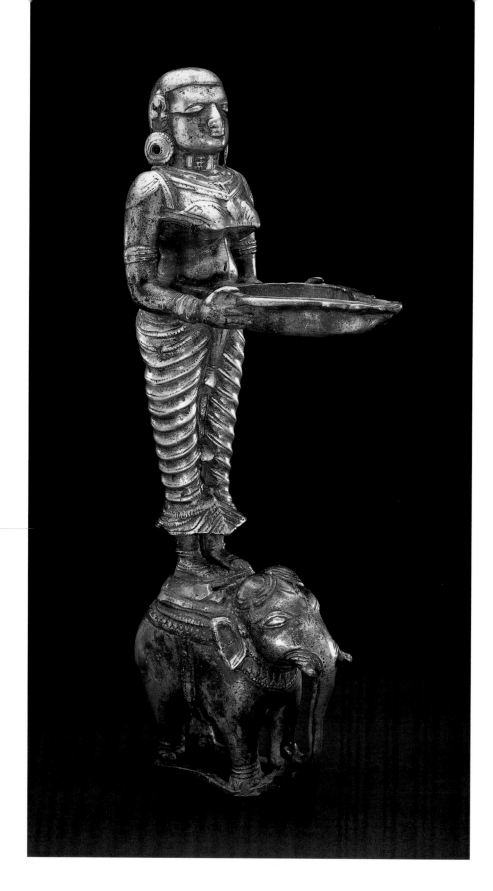

17.

Lakshmi *dipa*

Tamil Nadu, India
19th century
X2001.11.4

18.

Lakshmi *dipa*

Tamil Nadu, India
19th century
x2001.11.18

19.

Lakshmi *dipa*

Rajasthan, India
19th–20th century
X2001.11.22a,b

or *choli*, is highlighted with tight decorative patterns and a deep neckline. Sinuous bare arms with attenuated fingers hold the reservoir. Atop the goddess's right shoulder stands a small parrot with long tail feathers.

Most certainly from Rajasthan in northern India, the second example makes use of localized decorative qualities (fig. 19). With a heavier molding of form and a flattened silhouette, the female figure presents a striking contrast to the previous lamp. The pedestal is not integrated with the lamp. In addition, the rougher description of ornamental patterning suggests that the lamp was intended to be seen only frontally. Here Lakshmi stands regally on a small square plate with rectangular and relatively undefined feet. Again, she holds a reservoir in her outstretched arms, bestowing favor on the faithful. A cinched waistline and ample bosom betray her thinness. Striking floral patterns ornament her lower garment, which is divided vertically by a wide seam. Flares that begin at the waist and extend to the hemline exaggerate the perspectival quality of the figure, and the traditional attire imparts a vivacity to the goddess. She wears a tight *choli*, a wide decorated band necklace, and plentiful bracelets on her upper and lower arms. The size and depth of the oil reservoir are distinguished by the discrete detailing seen in the patterning of the figure's garments. The facial features are a study in hyperbole. *Darshan*, or the process by which the devotee actually "sees" the goddess, and the Goddess "sees" the devotee, is the most important function of such lamp images. Thus Devi's protruding eyes are enlarged, stretching from the bridge of her nose to the ear, although they contain only narrowly defined pupils. A sharp but wide nose balances the face while a diminutive mouth appears to be grinning. The figure's tresses have been cropped along the crown of her head, while two flared plaits descend from behind the ears mimicking the lateral expanse of her lower garment.

In each of the Lakshmi *dipa* considered here, the reflectivity of the metal; the posture, gaze, and accoutrements of the figure; and the manner is which light would be framed are intended to keep the focus of the faithful from straying. Crafting such elegant images of the Goddess was a means by which regional identity was strengthened among members of the community.

The Hanging Lamp: Suspension of Light

Hanging lamps, sometimes called chain lamps, may have originated from as far afield as ancient Greece or Rome, entering South Asia from the early ports of Arikamedu and Mammallapuram (both near present-day Chennai, Tamil Nadu). Used primarily in a temple context, the chain lamp cast its light broadly, and in so doing extended spiritual agency. Much like the other lamp types, it served as a backdrop to images placed before it on the altar. A collection of these hanging lamps within a temple setting would have generated a tremendous play of light and shadow over walls, ceilings, floors, and the eager faces of devotees.

The earliest lamp in the Pal Collection is a bronze Dongson lamp from Vietnam (fig. 20).[29] The lamp, which may have been intended to hang, includes a

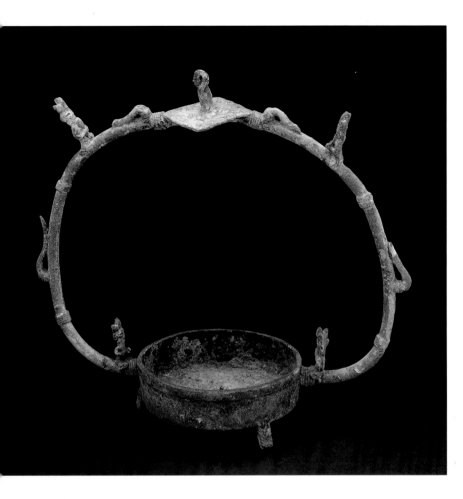

deep circular reservoir attached to a handle that is shaped like a hoop. Along the
edges of the handle are a series of small figures playing what appear to be flutes. They
are unified by spaced vertical striations that allude to rope. The formal design for the
lamp could have been modeled upon basketwork from the same region, indicating
fairly modest origins.

An early eleventh- to twelfth-century Khmer bronze from the Angkor period
in Cambodia depicts a kneeling female in the center of a lotus flower, the petals of
which are gently curled at the edges (fig. 21). The positioning of the Goddess in the
center of the lotus signifies that her powers are reflected in the pool of oil around
her. We might think of this as being a representation of the very site from which the
deity Lakshmi is said to have emerged, seated on a lotus in a churning ocean of milk.
The knees of the figure are separate from the ground upon which she sits. Although
some details are difficult to discern due to a thick patina, she appears to wear a cloth
around her hips, gathered about the waist. Her slightly down-turned face with open
eyes gives her a placid appearance. The hairstyle is one common to the period, with a
flat plait across the upper forehead. Her right arm is bent at the elbow and rests atop

her thigh with an upraised open palm in *abhaya mudra*, the hand gesture adopted by followers of Buddhism to imply fearlessness or renunciation.

Two hanging lamps in the collection come from East Java. One, which is of uncertain date, features a remarkably animated demon grimacing and seated among four burners (fig. 22). The other (fig. 23) is an important small bronze offering lamp attributed to the Majapahit period with a two-dimensional image of a horse within an arched frame. Poised between two separate oil reservoirs, the form of the horse would have been repeated by distinctive shadows cast in all directions. The knob-like protuberance at the top of the thin frame, suggests how this lamp may once have been hung.

A remarkable nineteenth- or twentieth-century hanging lamp from Nepal—a temple to be hung within the temple—seems to symbolize the notion of an undying light present within the sacred architecture of South Asia (fig. 24). The combining of rigid architectural forms with the fluidity of organic motifs characterizes all the Nepalese lamps in the Pal Collection. This lamp is an architectural exercise that includes resplendent burners with scalloped edges that are surmounted by figures of Ganesha, a two-story temple with columned loggia, and hanging leaf pendants.

21.

Hanging lamp in the shape of an open lotus flower with kneeling female

Cambodia
Angkor period, circa 12th
  century
Bronze
X2001.11.91

22.

Hanging lamp with demonic
guardian figure standing
in an open chest surrounded
by snakes

East Java, Indonesia
Date uncertain
X2001.11.94

Symmetrically composed on all four sides, this temple form with its raised plinth and
the addition of columned antechambers and balconies is common to northern India
and the Kathmandu Valley. The presence of peacocks at each corner of the lower level
of the lamp suggests welcome and the bestowing of wealth, which are associated with
the goddess Lakshmi.

　　A heavy, yet graceful, lamp from Kerala (fig. 25) was obviously hung as a focal
point within a temple, as suggested by the size of the chain and the diameter of the
reservoir. It takes the form of a large offering plate or bowl with a wide handle. The

23.

Hanging lamp with
winged horse

East Java, Indonesia
Attributed to Majapahit
    period, 14th century
Bronze
X2001.11.92

reservoir contains an illegible inscription in Malayalam, the state language of Kerala,
along one quarter of its interior edge. Symmetrical patterns on the widest portion of
the handle feature a design of raised triangular flames. At the center of the reservoir
are the naturalistic figures of an elephant and rider poised atop a pedestal. The elephant
is depicted with outstretched ears, a lazy tail, small protruding tusks, and a drooping
trunk. The rider grasps a ridged stick in one hand, while his other hand is firmly
planted behind his body. An incised garment rests loosely about his waist. The figure's
face is stoic but engaged.

24.

Hanging lamp in the form
of a temple

Nepal
19th–20th century
X2001.11.51

25.

Hanging lamp with elephant
and rider

Kerala, India
18th–19th century
X2001.11.88

26.

In the spirit of devotion, worshippers place their hands in the cool flames of burning camphor.

Photograph by Stephen P. Huyler, Manarashala, Alappuzha District, Kerala, 2003.

The Arati *Lamp: Menageries of Light*

Puja is a dynamic form of worship in which an individual, through prayer and the performance of the *arati* ritual respectfully beholds and experiences connection with the deity.[30] All the senses are engaged, and the individual in his or her home or the *pujari* within a temple moves the *arati* lamp—grasped firmly in the right hand—in a clockwise direction in front of the image of a deity. The lamp is first made to circle in front of the head of the image, then the central portion, and finally the base or feet. Typically, the person performing *puja* will ring a small ceremonial bell continuously while the *arati* lamp is flourished. *Arati* may also be performed with an incense holder or with small bricks of camphor lit upon a tray. After the tray has been presented to the deity, it is passed before the devotees who wave their hands through the fire and then spread this divine energy to their heads (fig. 26).[31] Stephen Huyler notes that "The fragrant flame represents the brilliant presence of the deity. Contact with the fire is believed to purify and elevate the devotee's soul, allowing it to merge with the magnificence of the Divine; at the same time, the energy of the Absolute unknowable deity is transformed and channeled into palpable connection with the devotee."[32]

27.

Maharashtra, India
19th century
X2001.11.2

28.

Rajasthan, India
20th century
X2001.11.26a-c

29.

Incense holder with Shiva's bull

South India
18th century
X2001.11.69

30.

Kulu, Himachal Pradesh, India
19th century
X2001.11.30

31.

Kulu, Himachal Pradesh, India
19th century
X2001.11.31

Arati lamps are often characterized by multiple reservoirs. Wicks are soaked in ghee or oil, placed in the reservoirs of the lamp, and then lit. In many instances, the handle is constructed so that the lamp in effect mediates between the devotee and the deity. In one instance a beautiful maiden, who may be identified as Lakshmi, seems to appear as intercessor between devotee and deity, and in the second, a peacock seems to fulfill this role (figs. 27, 28). Each of these lamps includes five reservoirs, a type referred to as *pancharati* (five flames) or *panchapradip* (five lamps), pointing to the significance of numerology in their design.[33] In an intricate *arati* incense holder from South India (fig. 29), the bull who is the *vahana* of Shiva is posed under an arch, as a secondary carrier of the devotee's prayers. An array of incense sticks would have been placed along the outer edge of the arch. The form of this incense holder resembles that of *arati* lamps found throughout South Asia.

32.

Incense holder

Gujarat, India
19th–20th century
X2001.11.10

Several *arati* lamps employ the image of an animal as an essential design component. Two lamps in the collection from the mountainous Kulu District in Himachal Pradesh in northwest India (figs. 30, 31) feature monkeys, and one of them (fig. 31) is an *arati* lamp. On the one hand, the monkey's quick and mischievous nature can be likened to the equally swift appearance and disappearance of light. On the other, like the Hindu monkey deity Hanuman, the light and warmth of the ritual fire during *arati* symbolize unfaltering commitment. Other examples are also animated by the physical traits of the animal upon which the design of the lamp is based. An incense burner from Gujarat takes the form of a peacock and is crafted with numerous receptacles for incense sticks along the rim of a disc. Once lit, the incense would create a fan of smoldering "feathers" of light (fig. 32). As with the elegant peacock *arati* lamp described above (see fig. 28), here the bird as an earthly representative of Lakshmi serves as an intercessor in the quest for good fortune.[34] *Arati* lamps also incorporate animals without reference to divinity, as may be seen in a tall nineteenth-century lamp from western Nepal with a lid in the form of a rooster (fig. 33). Crafted with restrained whimsy, the rooster stands atop a pedestal comprised of thin hammered iron.

33.

Lamp with rooster

Western Nepal
19th century
Iron
x2001.11.72a,b

34.

Maharashtra, India
20th century
X2001.11.53

The oil cups on this lamp
surround the rim of a larger
dish, used for cakes of incense.

A large Maharashtran *arati* lamp features an ingenious swiveling handle, allowing the devotee to cast a wide arc of light (fig. 34). The lamp's circular goblet is supported by a bell-shaped pedestal. The arched handle features Shaivite iconography including Shiva's *vahana*, a bull, venerating a lingam (the stylized phallic symbol associated with worship of Shiva) that is protected by a serpent, or *naga*, with an open hood. Behind the large hood of the upright *naga* are two small receptacles for incense sticks. Within the wide reservoir of the lamp, near its upper edge, is a deep-set shelf. Five separate oval burners are attached to the reservoir's outer edge. When used as part of an *arati* ritual, this swiveling lamp with its flames and incense may possibly have disappeared within a canopy of light. As D. G. Kelkar suggests, the flames of the *arati* lamp represent "the soul of the devotee which is offered to the deity. It is rekindled with the divine light of the Creator, Preserver and Destroyer."[35]

FESTIVALS OF LIGHT

The Hindu and Buddhist years are punctuated by a series of events in which aspects of spiritual life are embraced.[36] These are occasions when conventional notions of time and space are suspended. Shops and institutions close. Families purchase special clothing and furniture. Everyday life is put to the side in order to reenact long-standing compacts with the divine (figs. 35, 36).

In South and Southeast Asia, the light of lamps forms the focus of many of these important celebrations. Foremost among these are Navaratri, Karthigai, and Dipavali (Divali, Diwali). Held between October and December, these three celebrations deploy the lamp as an active symbol, a vehicle, and a beacon to which celebrants are drawn. As in Western holidays where the presence of lights informs popular culture and thought, the meaning of the lamp is extended in South Asian contexts to encompass multiple traditions and ideologies.

35.

Women place 1,008 ghee-filled clay lamps on a *kolam* representing a lotus, symbol of the Goddess. The completed lotus with all lamps in place may be seen in figure 36.

Photograph by Stephen P. Huyler, Samayapuram, Tiruchirappalli District, Tamil Nadu, 2003.

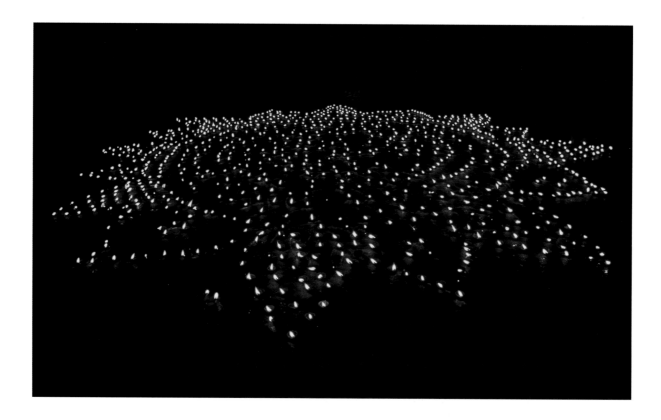

36.

The lotus pattern seen in figure 35 with all lamps in place.

Photograph by Stephen P. Huyler, Samayapuram, Tiruchirappalli District, Tamil Nadu, 2003.

Navaratri

Throughout the Indian Subcontinent the nine-day Navaratri festival—forming part of a longer period of fourteen nights of commemoration—assumes different aspects depending upon region and locale. Observed during the month of Aswin (September–October), the primary aim of the festival and its attendant rituals is to win the favor of Devi in order to obtain prosperity and good health for the following year. It is a festival of new beginnings, and as such, it exalts the bringing of light to the darkness of the past. Particularly in Gujarat, benevolent manifestations of the goddesses Lakshmi, Sarasvati, and Durga are worshipped. Performative aspects of the festival are as important as the mythic narratives that coincide with its celebration.

Throughout the evening and into the late nights of the nine days of Navaratri in Gujarat, people gather to perform the Garbha, a dance of epic proportion.[37] Wearing garments in shades of orange, blue, brown, white, and red, purchased especially for the occasion, participants follow an initial dancer who establishes the pace and the steps. Accompanied by musicians, the number of dancers gradually increases, as do the number of steps. With every footstep, the faithful honor the Goddess, whose image is situated at the center of their dance circle. The Garbha fuses its participants, who are coupled with standard foot and hand movements, into an ever-evolving system of dark and light. At the conclusion of the last dance each night, the participants gather at the image of Devi, while a chosen person performs a benediction or an *arati*

37.

As part of the annual autumnal Durga *puja*, an elaborate arrangement of 108 lamps is lit before the image in the Pal home near Kolkata.

Photograph mid-1990s.

ritual with lamps and censors to engage her. The heat generated by the vibrant dancing circle has been transferred to the lamp and its carrier as an offering to Devi. Light thus springs from the intersection of the body and devotion.

Lamps also figure in the events of the Navaratri festival wherein aspects of Durga, Lakshmi, and Sarasvati are acknowledged and welcomed into the home. Nine *saktis*, or forces of Devi, are worshipped in nine different forms, each of them requiring a specific lamp depending on the day.[38] The different stages of spiritual progress are reflected in the sequence of celebrations during Navaratri. During the first three days, Durga is worshipped (fig. 37). Correspondingly, Lakshmi is revered during the next three days. The last three days of Navaratri are dedicated to worshipping Sarasvati, who becomes the embodiment of knowledge through the Ayudha Puja. This *puja*, which is actually performed on the tenth night, is accompanied by complex *arati* rituals and pays homage to those implements used in one's livelihood.[39] On the preceding evening, the ninth night, it is traditional to place these implements on an altar with the images of Devi.

On the day following the Ayudha Puja, the faithful celebrate Lord Rama's destruction of Ravana, also known as Dusshera. This is a day of victory on which devotees worship Sarasvati, the goddess of learning, by placing books, writing implements, and lamps at the temple and their doorsteps—all of which are symbolic of the cultivation of knowledge.

Karthigai Dipam

Karthigai Dipam is celebrated for two days and marks the conclusion of a ten-day festival that is held in the month of Karthigai (October-November) in the state of Tamil Nadu in South India.[40] The faithful work diligently to prepare their homes to welcome the deities to the festival. New rice flour designs known as *kolam* are drawn nearly every day at the doorsteps of houses. In some cases they increase in complexity to the point where they resemble celestial maps upon which small lamps and candles are placed. Processions carrying images wend their way through the streets accompanied by countless lamps that light the path to nearby temples and sacred areas.

Where during Navaratri and Dipavali, lamps are vehicles for the cultivation of knowledge and beneficence, the light-centered rituals of Karthigai take on charged symbolic identities.[41] Lamps large and small are lit to propitiate the deities but on a grander scale than in other festivals. In the streets of Tiruvannamalai Town in Tiruvannamalai Sambuvarayar District, north of Chennai, thousands clamor to witness the lighting of a massive lamp at the main temple atop Arunachala Hill.[42] The temple houses a lingam constructed of igneous rock that is considered to be a natural emanation of Lord Shiva. It is believed that at one time Vishnu quarreled with Brahma over who was superior. In the midst of their fighting, Shiva, assuming the name Arunachala, appeared in the form of a column of fire so massive that it could not be circumscribed. Vishnu and Brahma agreed to resolve their disagreement by seeing who could find an end to the column first. Brahma became a bird and floated upward, while Vishnu assumed the guise of a boar and dug deep into the earth. Neither of the deities found the end of the pillar, and they came to realize that it was none other than Shiva himself. Shiva agreed to remain in the same spot as a lingam (known as the *agni linga*) immortalizing the needless conflict of Brahma and Vishnu. The name Arunachala, like Tiruvannamalai, may be literally translated as "holy fire hill." Every year during the Karthigai festival, thousands of earthen and metal lamps are lit, as well as a massive bonfire atop the hill, to commemorate this event—each flame symbolizing in miniature the fire lingam.

A requisite for Tamil brahmins, the Karthigai festival is dominated by the presence of women who make special prayers to appease the god of destruction, Lord Karthikeyan, also known as Lord Maruga,[43] who is thought to bring peace and harmony to households. When a woman is to be married, her parents will give her a number of lamps and, as noted above, her mother-in-law often gives her a lamp of Lakshmi on an elephant to promote fertility (see fig. 17). The gift of lamps—of light—is thought to cement familial bonds, especially those between brother and sister. These lamps are then lit every year at thresholds and windows in front of the house during the Karthigai festival, one after another, during the full moon. They are often set within *kolam* designs drawn outside the house in order to entice Devi to visit the household. Special offerings of rice and pulses, called Neyvedham, are presented among the lamps.

38.

During Dipavali women carry lamps to the holy Ganges River to perform *puja*.

Photograph by Stephen P. Huyler, Varanasi, 2002.

Dipavali

When in early autumn or late summer children begin to draw and paint simple patterns at their doorways or along curbs, it is often a sign that Dipavali is approaching. These drawings foreshadow the small footprints that will adorn the floors and walls of houses and the colorful *rangoli* designs that will decorate doorways and window ledges during the festival. *Rangoli*—which are known as *kolam* in South India or *alpana* in the state of Bengal—are drawn with rice flour and vibrant *kumkum* powders.[44] These beguiling designs are often further ornamented by lamps set within them.

Dipavali is the Hindu New Year, and it is predominantly a celebration of Lakshmi, the goddess of wealth and prosperity (although the emphasis varies regionally as will be discussed below). It is said that once Lakshmi was guided by a slender ray of light while traveling through the darkness. In return she bestowed blessings upon all those who lit lamps for her. Lamps are thus kept burning every night of the Dipavali festival (fig. 38). Without the aid of a lamp to dispel the shadows, the beneficent goddess would be unable to discern the direct pathway into the heart of the home. The lamps signify the end of a dark period, or *yuga*, and the dawning of a new and propitious one.

Dipavali commences twenty days after Dusshera on Amavasya, the fifteenth day of the Hindu month of Karttik (October-November).[45] The five-day celebration is universal, uniting Hindus throughout the subcontinent and in the diasporas. Even in countries where there are very small populations of Hindus, Dipavali will be celebrated. No matter what the locale, city streets and village pathways during these five days become conduits through which the deities are proclaimed and welcomed.

The perception of the significance or origin of the festival differs in the various regions of India. In North India it is thought of as a celebration of the homecoming of Rama and marked with triumphal marches and temple processionals. In Bengal it is associated with the goddess Kali manifested as Durga. In western India Lakshmi is honored with dancing and feasting. Fireworks, however, are common to all these celebrations. They mark the triumph of good, their tremulous blasts and bursts of colorful light reducing evil to ashes.

Each of the days of Dipavali has its own special rituals relating to particular mythological events. The first day, or Dhanteras, marks the suspension of everyday activities and commemorates Rama's return to Ayodhya after fourteen years of exile. Lamps are lit and kept burning throughout the night in adoration of Yam, the god of death. This recalls the story of a young, newly married prince who was prophesied to die from a snake's bite on the fourth night of his marriage. His young wife saved him from his fate by lighting innumerable lamps and creating vast displays of gold and jewelry. When Yam arrived in the guise of a serpent to claim the prince's life, he was blinded by the light and beguiled by the songs and stories of the young princess who kept him awake the whole night and cheated him of his prey.

The second day is known as Narakchaturdashi and recalls the killing of the demon Narakasura by Lord Krishna. As this is the first moment that the goddess Lakshmi is formally acknowledged, it is considered an auspicious occasion on which to make lamp offerings to the deity. This propitiation continues into the third day, which is called Lakshmi Puja and is solely devoted to the goddess. During the fourth day, Padwa or Varsha Pratpipada, prayers are offered in temples for divine protection in the New Year. The fifth and final day is sometimes called "Bhaiya-Dooj" and is a time when gifts are exchanged among family members, especially between brother and sister. The culmination of Dipavali celebrations is the awakening of Lord Vishnu from a four-month-long slumber. This is the season when the land has cooled from the tremendous heat of summer. Lamps are placed along roadsides and doorways to guide Rama and Lakshmi home after their arduous journey.

Lamps, in all of the festivals described here as well as numerous others, are a means of paying obeisance to the deities for the attainment of prosperity, knowledge, and peace. The light of the lamp, while a signal of safety and comfort, ensures the continued presence of Devi within the home, street, and temple. Lamps are therefore maintained throughout the evening and night as it is thought that bad fortune will come to those who allow the lamps to be extinguished before dawn of the next day. As darkness unfolds, the flickering of lamps, in front of every door, in the windows of houses and businesses, reminds all who witness their luminous splendor of the constant renewal of life.

CONCLUSION: FIAT LUX

One speaks of the lamp and the light it proffers simultaneously. Divine apparatus, symbol, arbiter of transformation, all of these labels might be applied to the lamp without fully accounting for its significance in the context of South and Southeast Asia. The lamps illustrated here are vibrant sculpture, crafted so that they might serve in any location to facilitate seeing and being seen by the divine. Each lamp presented in this volume contains a fragment of the unknowable, and all of them sustain and frame light, if momentarily, in order to focus attention on the deities. The act of *puja* confers light into the darkness of being; through its repetition knowledge is accessed. Some lamps, like the *dipa stambha* assume the role of a marker or beacon for the faithful. Similarly, hanging lamps provide a luminous screen between the altar and the devotee, mediating and serving as symbols of hope and promise.

Nearly every ritual—whether performed in a temple, in the office, or in the home—attempts to secure the limitless energy of the divine feminine. As craftsmen have attempted to define the potential of light, they have also envisioned Devi in her own right. Lakshmi *dipa* allow one to catch sight of and be regarded by Devi. The substance of light—effortlessly carried in deep reservoirs held by strong hands—animates the "Goddess," making her the personification of light itself. Yet it is the lamps used in the *arati* ritual that open the door to a corporeal experience of Devi. The *arati* lamp in all of its guises permits the greatest intimacy between the human and the divine.

One need not look any further to comprehend the timelessness of the lamp than a ritual that is often performed along the banks of rivers large and small throughout South and Southeast Asia, including the most sacred bodies of water, the Ganges and Kaveri Rivers in India. Hundreds of small lamps, made from folded leaves or pieces of clay and a wick in oil, are gently placed into the current (fig. 39). These are sent out on the water as *devadanam*, or gifts to the gods, with a wish or a promise attached. Some say that if the little lamp reaches the far side of the river without diminishing, then the wish will be granted. Others suggest these lamps are messages guided by light and sent to the ancestors.[46] After a moment, the river

39.

Prayers in the form of lighted lamps are released in the holy Ganges River.

Photograph by Stephen P. Huyler, Varanasi, 2001.

becomes a reflection of the night sky, its swiftly moving points of light transformed into constellations. Just as small flickering lamps in the sky have been appropriated for centuries to guide the wayward home, so the divine light of lamps like those illustrated in this book continues to serve as a spiritual guide for the peoples of South and Southeast Asia.

1. Vedic literature is thought to have influenced the expansion of Shaivism and Vaishnavism after the establishment of the Shunga dynasty in 185 BCE. It is not until after the second century CE, when the songs of worship, or Vedas, by the Dravidian poet Veda Vyasa, were transcribed in Sanskrit, that a more formalized Vedic principle of worship was established. See Basham (1967).

2. Agni will also be shown to have a threefold nature with three births, three heads, and three faces. Like Surya, he represents one of the first notions of an Indian trinity. Buddhism refers to Marichi as an incarnation of Vairochana who is often depicted with three faces, referring to morning, noon, and night.

3. Numerous references to sun worship occur throughout the *Puranas.* The *Ramayana* describes sun worship through the establishment of mantras and ceremonies. Sun temples, described by ancient travelers, are seen today throughout the subcontinent including Arasavilli and Konark in Orissa; Dakshinaarka Temple in Gaya, Bihar; Suryanaar Koyil in Tirumangalakkudi, Tamil Nadu; Modhera in Gujarat; Ranakpur in Rajasthan; Surya Pahar in Golapara, Assam; and Unao in Madhya Pradesh. The ruins of early sun temples are also found in Martand in Kashmir as well as in Multan, Pakistan. Many of these temples bear iconography that suggests their origins in Asia Minor.

4. The linguistic origins of the name Agni are Indo-European (Latin, *igni-s*) and may have initially suggested the term *agile* coming from the root *ag*, "to drive" (Latin, *ago*; Greek, *hágo*; Sanskrit, *ag*).

5. Gangoly also proposes that the practice of using lamps within the Christian liturgical tradition may have originated from a functional necessity within the darkened catacombs. See Gangoly (1916, 142).

6. Further discussion of the Shunga-style railing detailing the "Dream of Maya" is conceptually important as analogous sculptural motifs are used across the subcontinent. See Sharma (1994). For a discussion of how visual narratives structure one's perception of the Bharhut stupa complex, see Dehejia (1998).

7. Chandraketugarh has been shown to have flourished from the third century BCE until the conclusion of the Sena period in 1250 CE. For the most comprehensive examination of this vital and complex archaeological site, see Haque (2001). See also a special issue devoted to early terra-cotta sculpture in India in *Marg* 52 (September 2002).

8. O. C. Gangoly contends that these figures represent donors of the temple, irrespective of their gender, since "both sexes share a common origin, birth from the womb of a woman" (Gangoly 1916, 142).

9. The Ashta Shakti Mandapam at the Indian temple city of Madurai, Tamil Nadu, for instance, includes lamp holders for 1,008 lamps, which are lit during festivals and other important occasions.

10. A number of other historians and ethnographers have elucidated metal-casting processes used by tribal craftsmen in India. See Grigson (1938); Elwin (1951); Reeves (1962); and Mukherjee (1978).

11. The terminology used to describe the craftsmen and their respective objects is often conflated with the region and materials used. Carol Radcliffe Bolon and Amita Vohra Sarin remark that "it is easy to confuse the identities of the similar yet different products made by these distinct groups of craftsmen…the Dhokra work of Bengal is named for the craftsmen; the products of some of the Orissan metal casters are known as Kondh bronzes, named after the Kond tribes that buy them," whereas Bastar works are labeled as "Bastar bronzes," but "known popularly in India as Dhokra work." Bolon and Sarin (1992, 44).

12. The state of Chhattisgarh was officially recognized in November 2000.

13. Bolon and Sarin (1992, 44).

14. Kramrisch (1968, 55). Bolon and Sarin also acknowledge the variation of themes generated by Bastar metalworkers working "within the parameters of style and technique traditional for generations and typical of the Bastar region" (1992, 43).

15. There are fourteen commonly found motifs/patterns used in the lost-wax process adapted by the Bastar: (1) braid pattern, or *benisut;* (2) diamond-shaped chain, or *pikad pan;* (3) rings, or *bhaunri jal;* (4) globule, ball-like pattern, or *duru;* (5) lateral lines; (6) zigzag; (7) sun and moon, or *ber and jon;* (8) notches and indentations; (9) circle with a dot in the center, or *bundia dhuru;* (10) wheat grain motif, or *gehun dana;* (11) flower of the bitter gourd, or *karela phool;* (12) a chain of side-by-side spiders, or *makri;* (13) eye of the maina bird, or *rami kajal;* (14) tiger's claws, or *bagnakha.* For further explanation of the casting process and the usage of these patterns, see Postel and Cooper (1999, 85). See also Bolon and Sarin (1992, 42–45, 49).

16. Bolon and Sarin (1992, 44).

17. Jaitly (1990, 44).

18. "The jar is called *kalasha*, because Vishvakarma made it from the different parts of each of the Devatas. It should be thirty-six fingers in breadth in its widest part and sixteen in height. The neck should be four fingers in breadth, the mouth six, and the base five. This is the rule for the design of the kalasha." *Mahanirvana Tantra*, reprinted in Coomaraswamy (1913, 140).

19. The wide girth of Ganesha (Vinayaka, Ganapati) is considered to symbolize the cosmos, while his head suggests a powerful intellect. Ganesha's symbolic mount, or *vahana*, the rat, represents equality among all creatures, large and small.

20. Pal (1969, 158). See also a brief discussion on the Tibetan borrowing from Christian sources in Pal (1991, 136).

21. There is abundant evidence that Indian artists created works for Tibetan patrons. For the integration of craft, patronage, and metaphysical symbolism in Tibetan sculpture, see Singer and Denwood (1997); Weldon and Singer (1999); Heller (1999); and Pal (2003).

22. Coomaraswamy (1913, 141).

23. The sacred tree, along with its attended shrine (*devasthana*) will be constantly worshipped by the community. "When the tree dies," Huyler continues, "the spot remains sacred. It is believed to be vibrant with the energies of innumerable pujas and will usually continue to be a focus of community worship, most often with a platform or building constructed where the tree stood" (1999, 102–5).

24. Coomaraswamy (1913, 141).

25. Gangoly (1916, 147).

26. While the tree motif is seen among many lamps, only two types of specific trees are ever constructed. The first, a peepul tree, or *asvattha*, is renowned throughout South Asia as one of the symbolic bastions of Vishnu. A more common tree used in metalwork and sculpture is the conically shaped pine tree.

27. Specifically, the Gonds form the majority of the Bastar peoples in Madhya Pradesh and Chhattisgarh. See Bolon and Sarin (1992, 36).

28. Bolon and Sarin (1992, 37).

29. The term "Dongson" refers to a late Bronze Age culture that flourished between circa 500 BCE and circa 200 CE in present-day Vietnam. It has subsequently been applied rather loosely to stylistically similar objects found throughout Southeast Asia, including the Indonesian archipelago, whose origins, dating, and relationship to the Dongson site in Vietnam are uncertain.

30. The flames themselves may be portentous for those using the *arati* lamp. Recounting a portion of the *Shilpa Shashtras* in Vedic literature, D. G. Kelkar quotes the *Purushottama Mahatmya*, whereby the color of the flame signified one's state of being, "Drying-up flames indicate the destruction of wealth; white flames indicate the waste of sustenance; flames that are very red indicate wars, and black flames indicate death" (1961, 18).

31. Camphor (*karpura*) is extracted from the pitch of the camphor tree. Huyler has described its "cold-burning" characteristics, "When lighted, it has the unique property of creating a bright, cool flame that leaves no residue or ash" (1999, 60).

32. (Huyler 1999, 60). For further discussion of the metaphysical components of *puja* and *arati* rituals, see Eck (1998).

33. Five burners or wicks are also common among South Indian lamps. The ubiquitous five-nozzle lamp, or *kuthu vilakku*, represents the five elements of nature: earth, water, fire, air, and space.

34. Verrier Elwin remarks that the Bastar Gonds use the image of the peacock in their rituals and metal-work as the bird's feathers are readily accessible. The form of the peacock among the Bastar and other tribal peoples, according to Elwin, is closely related to rituals of the dead and to communication with ancestors. See Elwin (1951, 154).

35. Kelkar (1961, 6).

36. It is important to note that the Hindu calendar, termed the Saka era after the period in which it was formulated, follows the lunar cycle. The Nepalese calendar, while nearly parallel, is referred to as the Bikram Sanbat and is marked with traditional Nepalese Hindu and royal events.

37. The following descriptions of the Navaratri festival are based on the author's personal experiences and observations in Navrangpura and old city zones of Ahmedabad, Gujarat, in 1999 and 2000.

38. The nine forms of Devi are: (1) Kumari, (2) Trimurti, (3) Kalyani, (4) Rohini, (5) Kalika, (6) Chandika, (7) Sambavi, (8) Durga, and (9) Subhadra. See Kinsley (1986) and Hawley and Wulff (1996).

39. It is unclear if the origins of this rite are associated with Sarasvati. *Ayudha* means "emblem," but in this instance it refers to arms and weapons.
40. Karthigai is the Tamil term that corresponds to Karttik in Sanskrit.
41. There are eleven primary types of lamps used during the Karthigai festival including: (1) perpetual lamp, or *thungavilakku*, (2) branch lamp, or *kilai vilakku*, (3) "lady with a lamp," or *pavai vilakku*, (4) hanging lamp, (5) hand lamp, or *kai vilakku*, (6) garland lamp or *torana vilakku*, (7) elephant lamp, or *gaja vilakku*, (8) pot lamp, or *karaha dipam*, (9) *bhajan* lamp, *bhajan* referring to devotional singing, (10) *chettiar* lamp, *chettiar* referring to a caste in Tamil Nadu, and (11) ground lamp, or *kuthuvilakku*.
42. Several recent visitors to the sites at Tiruvannamalai during this festival period have shared their experiences with me, and these descriptions form the basis of this section. I am grateful to Shagun Mehrotra and his family in Mumbai and Indore; Annapindi Ramesh; and Lakshmi Parthasarathy and her family in Chennai for their continued friendship and poetic observations of this festival, as well as others, during my various stays in India.
43. Lord Maruga is recognized as an intermediary between Vaishnavites and Shaivites among Tamil brahmins. His temples are built throughout South and Southeast Asia.
44. These drawings differ greatly in material, form, and design from region to region and among various societies. Some drawings are made only once a year, typically prior to Dipavali, whereas others are created for significant events throughout the year. For a rigorous examination and analysis of such designs throughout the Indian Subcontinent, see Huyler (1994).
45. The descriptions of the Dipavali festival presented here are based on my personal observations made between the years of 1997 and 2004 in a number of urban and rural locales in South and Southeast Asia, including India, Nepal, and Burma.
46. Compare this with the festival known as Loy Krathong, which is held in Thailand in November. Adults and children alike make *krathong*, or boats, of lotus flowers and paper, light them with a candle or incense, and place them in a river accompanied by a wish.

Catalog

Container Lamps

CAT. NO. 1

Indonesia
probably 18th–19th century
X2001.11.93

This unusual piece, in the form of a Roman lamp, came from Indonesia and was probably made during the Dutch colonial period.

CAT. NO. 2

South India
19th century
X2001.11.14a,b

The tail of a peacock, who rides a caparisoned horse, supports a small oil cup with a swiveling lid. The knob at the front of the peacock unscrews to provide access to the oil chamber inside the bird's body.

CAT. NO. 3

Rajasthan, India
19th century
x2001.11.81a,b

The hollow body of this elephant serves as an oil reservoir. The wick passes through a finial, which screws off so that the reservoir can be filled.

CAT. NO. 4

Bastar, Chhattisgarh, India
20th century
x2001.11.64a,b

Of the various animal-shaped container lamps from Bastar, this fish with a peacock finial is perhaps the most unusual.

CAT. NO. 5

Bastar, Chhattisgarh, India
20th century
X2001.11.62a,b

The hollow body of the large
peacock serves as a reservoir
for oil. The wick protrudes
directly through the top of the
removable finial, which bears
a second, smaller peacock.

CAT. NO. 6

Western Nepal
19th century
Iron
X2001.11.50

This lamp is typical of the
work of tribal groups in the
west of Nepal. The bird's head,
through which the wick passes,
can be screwed off to access the
oil reservoir in its body.

CAT. NO. 7

Bastar, Chhattisgarh, India
20th century
x2001.11.65a,b

The wick passes through the
removable finial of this lamp.
The shape of the container may
indicate Persian influence.

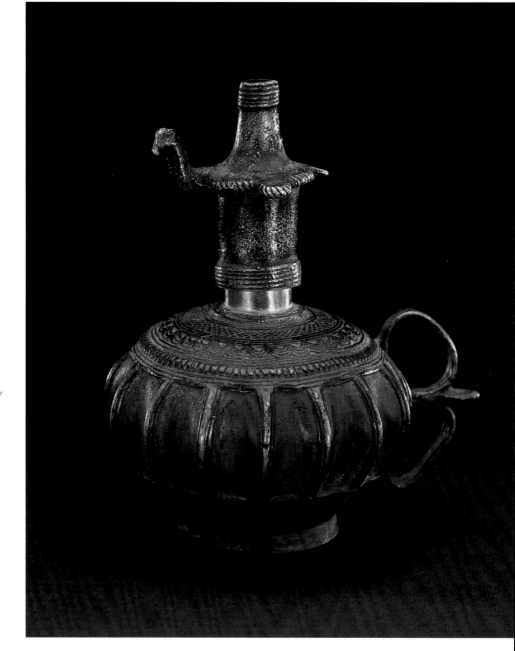

CAT. NO. 8

South India
19th century
X2001.11.15

Places for five wicks surround
this *dipa stambha*, which is
topped by a bird.

CAT. NO. 9

Bastar, Chhattisgarh, India
20th century
X2001.11.19

A peacock decorates the central
stambha of this lamp, and four
more birds perch at the rim of
the oil reservoir.

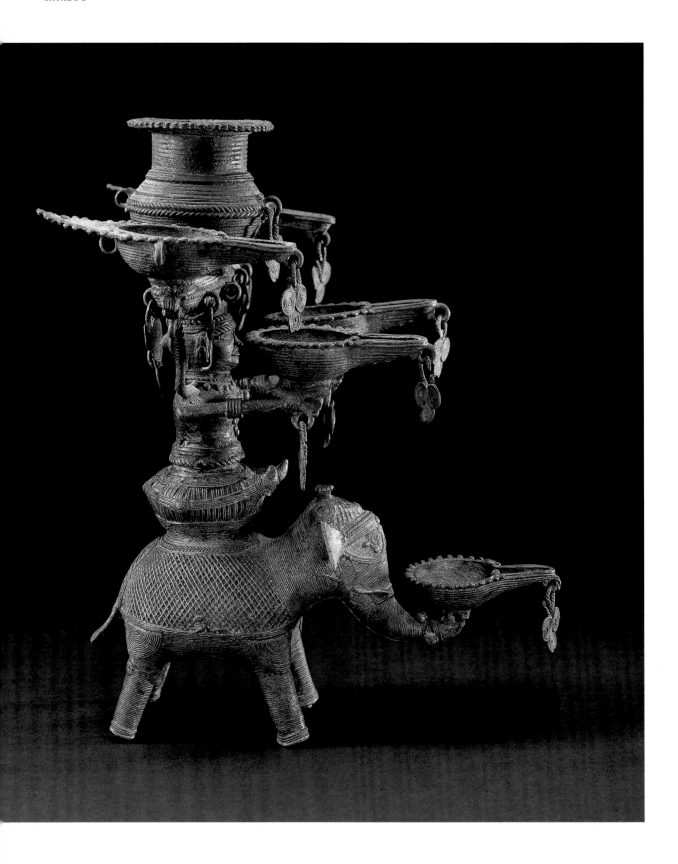

CAT. NO. 10

Bastar, Chhattisgarh, India
Mid-20th century
X2001.11.45

A goddess and the elephant
she rides provide support for
five oil burners. On top is
a small pot. The fine cross-
hatching and details are
typical of Bastar casting.

CAT. NO. 11

Orissa or Chhattisgarh, India
20th century
X2001.11.73

A horse carries a double-urn
shape. A hole runs down
the center of the entire figure
with no closure at the bottom,
indicating that it was intended
to hold a candle or an attach-
ment for a lamp.

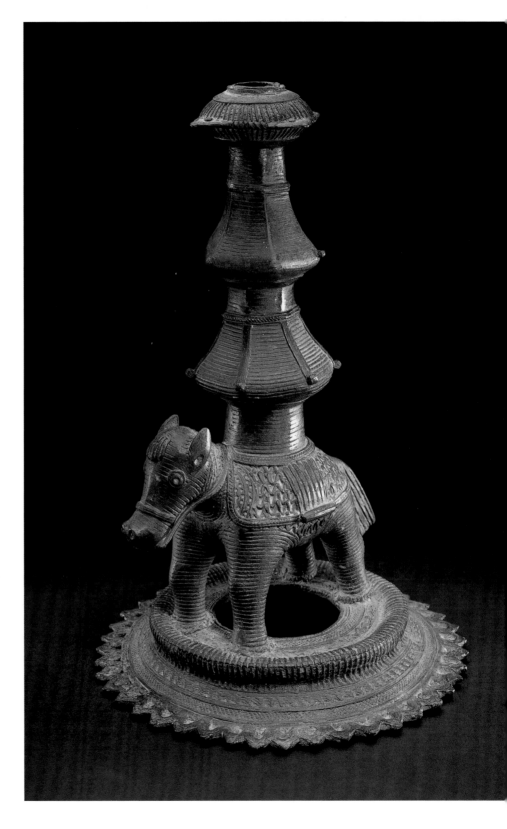

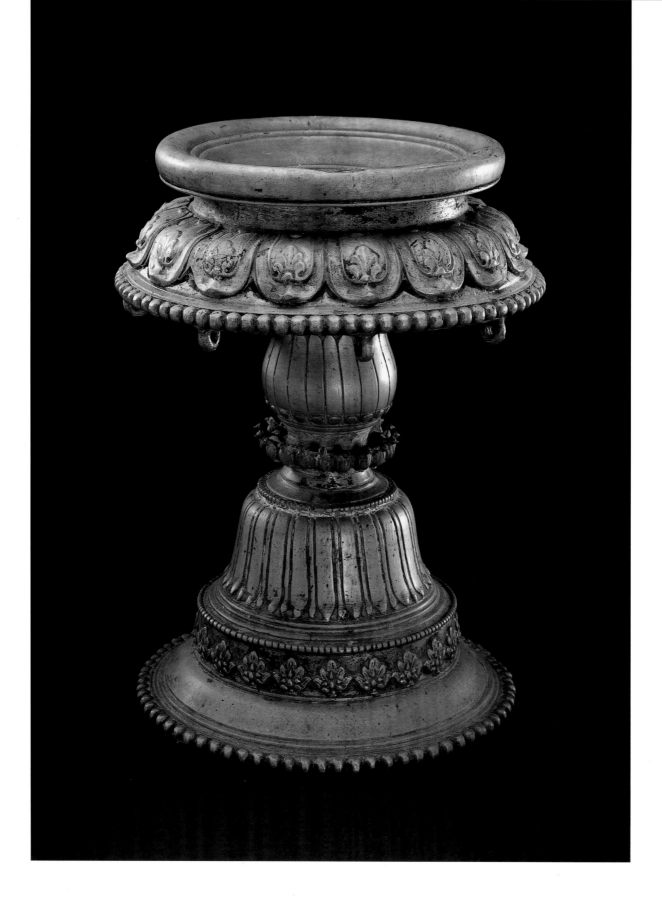

CAT. NO. 12 (LEFT)

Lamp base

Nepal
19th century
X2001.11.85

Offerings or small metal or
clay lamps could be placed on
the plate-like upper surface of
this lamp base. The marks on
the rim suggest that something
was once attached above the
plate, perhaps the burners of
the lamp.

CAT. NO. 13

Incense burner

Gujarat, India
19th–20th century
X2001.11.11

The hinged lid of this incense
burner lifts up to provide
access to the chamber inside.

CAT. NO. 14

Tamil Nadu, India
19th century
X2001.11.8a,b

This *dipa stambha* supports a
detachable array of seven small
oil cups.

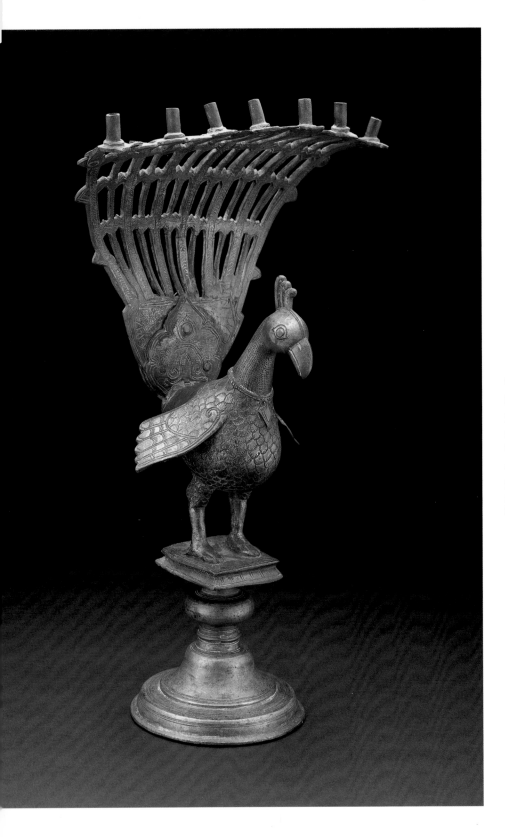

CAT. NO. 15

Incense burner

Rajasthan, India
20th century
X2001.11.12

This large and heavy peacock
is constructed to bear seven
sticks of incense on the tips of
its tail feathers

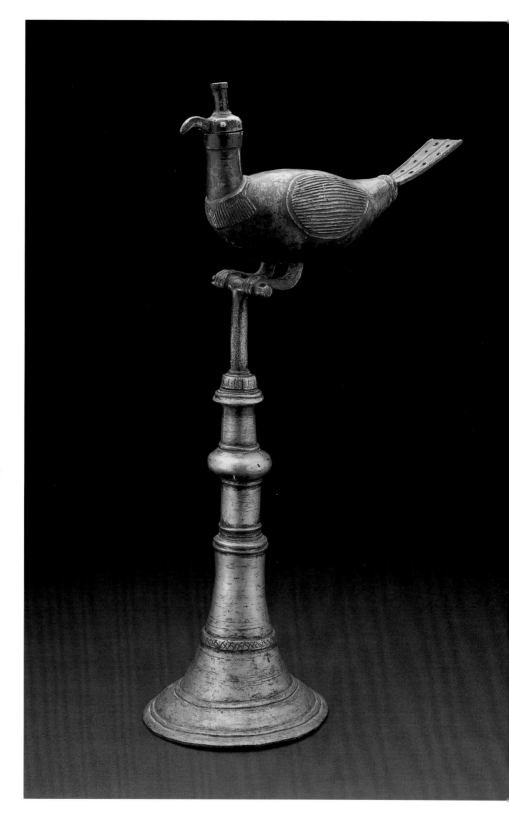

CAT. NO. 16

Western Nepal
20th century
X2001.11.70a,b

The bell in this *dipa stambha* has a clapper and rings with clear tones. Bells are often rung as part of the *arati* ritual. The body of the bird is hollow and serves as the oil reservoir, while the head is a screw-on cap with a hole in its center through which the wick passes.

CAT. NO. 17

Lamp or candleholder

Kerala, India
18th century
X2001.11.68a-c

This lamp from a Vaishnavite temple takes the form of a boat with rows of standing figures (eleven musicians on one side and five devotees on the other). Each figure has individual characteristics. At the center is

Garuda. The last figure before the bow appears to be Hanuman, and on the bow itself is a rider on a horse or bull. The cups now contain candle stubs, but in the past they could also have been used for oil and wicks.

The form of the lamp and an opening for a shaft at the bottom suggest that it was carried atop a *stambha*, or pole, of some sort.

CAT. NO. 18

Tamil Nadu, India
20th century
X2001.11.61

The leaping figures on the
base of this lamp are mythical
figures known as *vyala*.

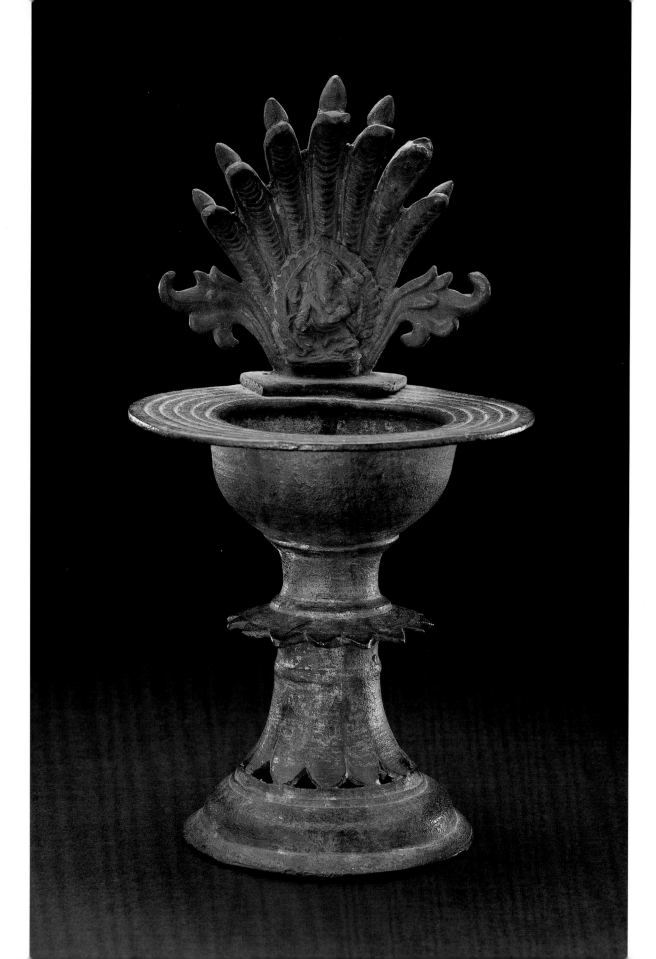

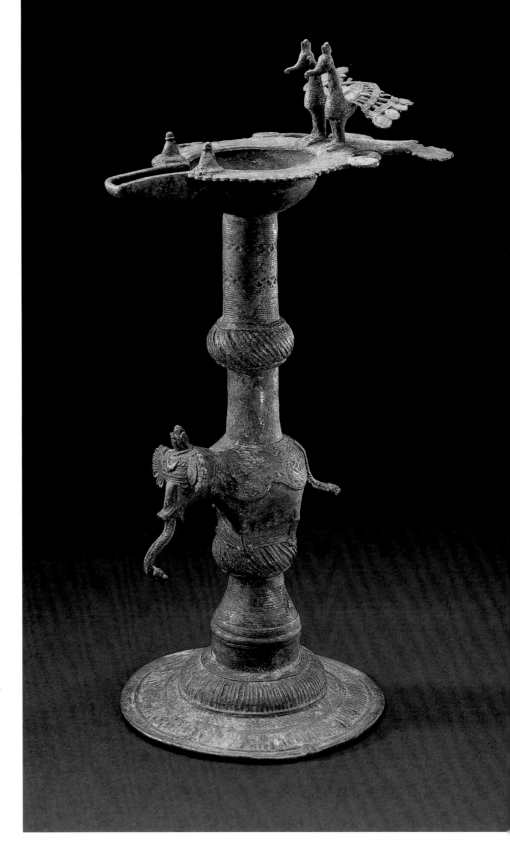

CAT. NO. 19

Madhya Pradesh, India
20th century
X2001.11.41

A figure of Ganesha presides
over the oil cup of this lamp,
under the shelter of a hood
formed of seven *naga*s.

CAT. NO. 20

Bastar, Chhattisgarh, India
20th century
X2001.11.57

An elephant dominates the
central *stambha* of this lamp,
while two peacocks face two
small lingams, or phallic symbols, on the rim of the oil cup,
which is formed in the shape of
a yoni, a stylized representation
of female genitalia.

Lakshmi *Dipa*

CAT. NO. 24 (LEFT)

South India
19th century
Iron
X2001.11.87

The hollow body of this heavy
rooster, which is designed to
hang by a chain, serves as an oil
storage reservoir. A small pin,
also in the form of a rooster,
can be removed to provide
access to the foot-shaped oil
pan at the base of the lamp.
The base has holes for holding
incense sticks and five "toes"
intended to hold wicks.

CAT. NO. 25

North India
20th century
Tin
X2001.11.40

This lamp from a Muslim
community was meant to
hang on a wall. It has six oil
cups suspended from a grid
of tin strips. The grid suggests
a cosmological diagram, or
yantra, although it may be
purely structural.

CAT. NO. 26

Nepal
20th century
Pewter
X2001.11.43

This lamp was designed to
hang on a wall.

CAT. NO. 27 (LEFT)

Incense burner

Rajasthan, India
19th century
X2001.11.66

The upper body of the peacock is hinged where it joins the handle of the burner and can be lifted up, allowing incense to be placed in the lower body. Once the lid is closed, the smoke rises through the holes in the upper body.

CAT. NO. 28

Rajasthan, India
19th century
X2001.11.6

This lamp's peacock-shaped handle supports an array of five oil cups. The round upper tray may have accommodated burning camphor.

CAT. NO. 29

Uttar Pradesh, India
20th century
X2001.11.49

The outstretched forelegs of this horse once held the burner for the lamp or possibly some device for holding incense.

97

CAT. NO. 30

Incense burner

Western India
19th–20th century
X2001.11.9

The handle of this stupa-shaped incense burner is decorated with a pair of peacocks. It also bears some lettering or symbols whose meanings are unclear. One of these, however, resembles the trident associated with Shiva.

CAT. NO. 31

India, possibly Karnataka
  or Maharashtra
19th century
X2001.11.34

The female figure on this lamp is elaborately dressed with a crown, pectoral, armlets, bangles, and a decorated braid down her back. A handle, now broken off, was once attached to the back of the figure and to the base.

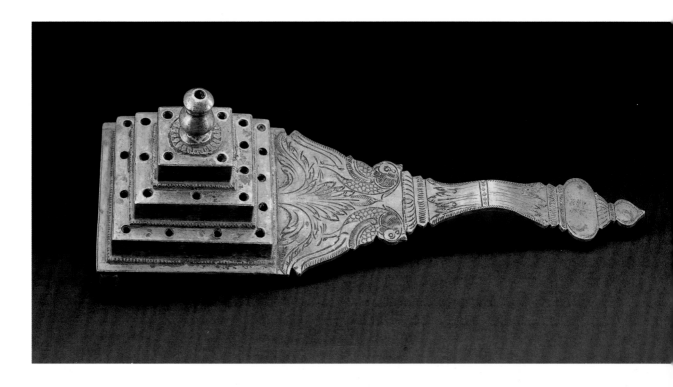

CAT. NO. 32

Incense burner

Western India
19th–20th century
X2001.11.67

A pair of peacocks grace the
handle of this ziggurat-shaped
incense burner. The finial rises
out of a lotus blossom.

CAT. NO. 33

Gujarat, India
19th century
X2001.11.3

The *naga* finial on the handle
of this lamp faces an array of
eight small oil burners.

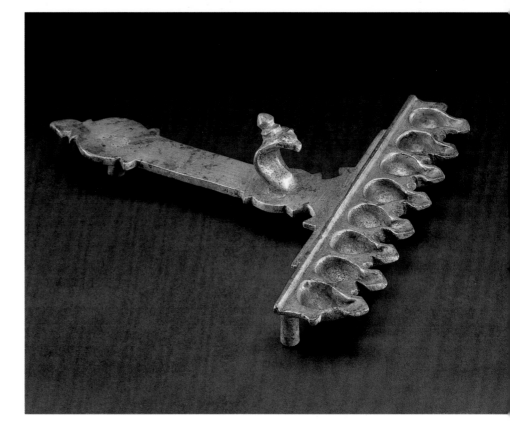

CAT. NO. 34 (LEFT)

Incense burner

Bastar, Chhattisgarh, India
20th century
X2001.11.75a,b

The incense stick holder, decorated with typical Bastar designs, is detachable from the base of this incense burner.

CAT. NO. 35

South India, possibly Karnataka
20th century
X2001.11.54

The star-shaped burner of this lamp accommodates five wicks. Like many *arati* lamps, it rests on two stupa-shaped bases.

CAT. NO. 36

Lamp with incense burner

South India, possibly
    Karnataka
19th century
X2001.11.77

The handle of this lamp bears a *naga*, with a flared hood, facing a miniature lingam, or phallic symbol. The main reservoir is intended for lamp oil, while three holes at the back of the *naga*'s hood are intended to support incense sticks.

CAT. NO. 37

Maharashtra, India
19th century
X2001.11.27

A female figure, bearing a tray
of five small burners, rides a
caparisoned elephant. A *naga*
tops the handle of this lamp.

CAT. NO. 38

Nepal
19th century
X2001.11.95

A warrior in a loincloth
supports the burner, which
is backed by a small figure
of Ganesha. The large, florid,
stupa-shaped snuffer is
attached to the lamp with
a *naga*-shaped handle.

Miscellaneous Lamps

CAT. NO. 39 (LEFT)

Tibet or Nepal
19th century
copper, brass
X2001.11.97a,b

This large butter lamp, probably from a Tibetan Buddhist temple, is made of hammered copper with added Chinese-inspired decorations of cast brass.

CAT. NO. 40

Madhya Pradesh, India
19th century
X2001.11.20

The bowl of this unusual lamp sits atop a cast head. The handle carries several symbols associated with the Hindu deity Shiva, including a lingam (phallic symbol), a bull, and a trident mark on the underside of the *naga's* hood.

CAT. NO. 41

Nepal
20th century
X2001.11.42

Parrots rise from the rim of this
lamp, while the upper part is
decorated with an amulet, sun
and moon symbols, and a V
indicating the Vaishnavite sect.

CAT. NO. 42

Tibet
18th–19th century
Iron
X2001.11.98

A large pair of tweezers is
attached by a chain to this
roughly forged iron lamp and
is intended to be used for
snuffing out the burning wick.

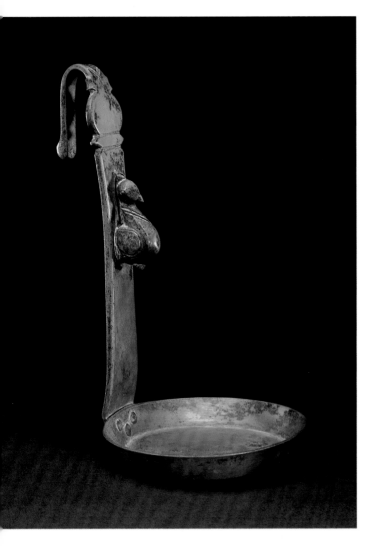

CAT. NO. 43

Lamp, ladle, or incense burner

Rajasthan, India
20th century
X2001.11.52

This ladle-like object may have
been used to transfer lamp oil
from a container. The ladle
could also function as a lamp
if wicks were placed in the
bowl, or as a platform for
burning incense.

CAT. NO. 44

Tamil Nadu, India
19th century
X2001.11.7

This lamp has two large bowls
for oil and a smaller upper
container that could have been
used for an additional wick or
for a lump of incense.

CAT. NO. 45

Lamp and incense burner

Bastar, Chhattisgarh, India
20th century
X2001.11.79

This elephant, with four riders
standing on the howdah, or
covered seat, shows the fine
detail typical of Bastar casting.
The oil lamp sits atop the
elephant's trunk, while the
howdah provides a platform
for burning incense.

List of Sanskrit Terms with Diacritical Marks

abhaya mudrā
ādivāsi
ālpanā
āratī
ārātrika
aśvattha
atithī
ātmā
āyūdha
darśan
devadānam
devasthāna
dhūṇa
dīp
dīpa
dīpak
dīpavṛiksha
diyā
dūta
garbha-gṛiha
ghī

grāmadevatā
gṛiha-pati
haṃsa
jīvanjyoti
karpūra
nāga
pañchapradīp
pañchāratī
pradīp
pūjā
pūjārī
rāga
rātri
sākshīn
śakti
saṃskāra
śrībalipura
triśūl
vāhana
vṛiksha
vyāla

References Cited

Alphonso-Karkala, John B., ed.
1971 *An Anthology of Indian Literature.* Harmondsworth: Penguin Books.

Basham, Arthur Llewellyn
1967 *The Wonder That Was India: A Survey of the History and Culture of the Indian Sub-Continent before the Coming of the Muslims.* London: Sidgwick & Jackson.

Besant, Annie, trans.
1967 *The Bhagavad-Gītā.* Vol. 19. 11th ed. Madras: The Theosophical Publishing House.

Bolon, Carol Radcliffe, and Amita Vohra Sarin
1992 "Bastar Brasses." *Asian Art* 5, no. 3: 34–51.

Coomaraswamy, Ananda
1913 *Arts and Crafts of India and Ceylon.* London: T. N. Foulis Inc.

Dehejia, Vidya
1998 "Circumambulating the Bharhut Stupa: The Viewers' Narrative Experience." In *Picture Showmen: Insights into the Narrative Tradition in Indian Art.* Edited by Jyotindra Jain. Mumbai: Marg Publications on behalf of National Centre for the Performing Arts.

Eck, Diana
1998 *Darśan: Seeing the Divine Image in India.* New York: Columbia University Press.

Elwin, Verrier
1951 *The Tribal Art of Middle India.* London: Oxford University Press.

Gangoly, O. C.
1916 "Southern Indian Lamps." *The Burlington Magazine for Connoisseurs* 29, no. 160 (July).

Grigson, Wilfred
1938 *The Maria Gonds of Bastar.* London: Oxford University Press.

Haque, Enamul
2001 *Chandraketugarh: A Treasure House of Bengal Terracottas.* Dhaka: The International Centre for Study of Bengal Art.

Hawley, John Stratton, and Donna Marie Wulff, eds.
1996 *Devi: Goddesses of India.* Berkeley: University of California Press.

Hazra, R. C.
1958 *Studies in the Upapurāṇas.* Vol. 1. Calcutta: The Sanskrit College.

Heller, Amy
1999 *Tibetan Art: Tracing the Development of Spiritual Ideals and Art in Tibet, 600–2000 A.D.* Milan: Jaca Book.

Huyler, Stephen P.
1994 *Painted Prayers: Women's Art in Village India.* New York: Rizzoli.
1999 *Meeting God: Elements of Hindu Devotion.* New Haven: Yale University Press.

Jaitly, Jaya
1990 *The Craft Traditions of India.* New Delhi: Lustre Press Pvt. Ltd.

Kelkar, D. G.
1961 *Lamps of India.* Pune: The Publications Division, Ministry of Information and Broadcasting.

Kinsley, David
1986 *Hindu Goddesses: Visions of the Divine Feminine in Hindu Religious Tradition.* Berkeley: University of California Press.

Kramrisch, Stella
1968 *Unknown India: Ritual Art in Tribe and Village.* Philadelphia: Philadelphia Museum of Art.

Kumari, Ved
1973 *The Nilamata Purana.* Vol. 2. Srinagar: J & K Academy of Art, Culture and Languages.

Monier-Williams, Monier
1979 *The Sanskrit-English Dictionary.* Oxford: Oxford University Press.

Mukherjee, Meera
1978 *Metal Craftsmen of India.* Calcutta: Anthropological Survey of India.

Pal, Pratapaditya
1969 *The Art of Tibet.* New York: The Asia Society.
1991 *Art of the Himalayas: Treasures of Nepal and Tibet.* Manchester, Vt.: Hudson Hills Press.
2003 *Himalayas: An Aesthetic Adventure.* Chicago: Art Institute of Chicago.

Postel, Michel, and Zarine Cooper
1999 *Bastar Folk Art: Shrines, Figurines, and Memorials.* Mumbai: Franco-Indian Research.

Reeves, R.
1962 *Cire Perdue Casting in India.* New Delhi: Crafts Museum.

Sharma, Ramesh Chandra
1994 *Bharhut Sculptures.* New Delhi: Abhinav Publications.

Singer, Jane Casey, and Phillip Denwood, eds.
1997 *Tibetan Art: Towards a Definition of Style.* London: Laurence King Publications.

Tagore, Rabindranath
1968 *Gītabitān.* Vol. 2. Calcutta: Bishvabharati.

Weldon, David, and Jane Casey Singer
1999 *The Sculptural Heritage of Tibet: Buddhist Art in the Nyingjei Lam Collection.* London: Laurence King Publications.

About the Author

Sean Anderson is a Fellow of the American Academy in Rome and a doctoral candidate in the Department of Art History at the University of California, Los Angeles. His dissertation concerns the making of modern spaces in colonial Asmara, Eritrea. A graduate of Cornell and Princeton Universities with degrees in architectural design and the history of architecture, he has worked as a practicing architect as well as a visiting professor of architectural design, history, and theory in Ahmadabad, India.

Staff List